DEVELOPMENT DIALOGUE

DEVELOPMENT DIALOGUE
Thoughts on Socio Economic Issues

Manu N Kulkarni

GYAN

ISBN: 978-81-212-1208-3

Price: ₹ 550

First Published 2014

Published by

Gyan Publishing House
23, Main Ansari Road
Daryaganj, New Delhi-110002
Phones: 23282060, 23261060
Fax : 91-11-23285914
E-mail: books@gyanbooks.com

Laser Typesetting : Shah Computer Graphics, Delhi

Printed at: Chawla Offset Printers, Delhi

Cataloging in Publication Data—DK

Courtesy: D.K. Agencies (P) Ltd. <docinfo@dkagencies.com>

Kulkarni, Manu N.

Development dialogue-thoughts on socio economic issues / Manu N. Kulkarni.

p. cm.

Includes index.

ISBN 9788121212083

1. Demographic transition. 2. Community development. 3. Community development--India. 4. Quality of life. 5. Quality of life--India. 6. India--Social conditions. 7. India—Economic conditions. I. Title.

DDC 304.62 23

To
My Wife Vijayalaxmi
For Her
Compassion Care and Concern

Contents

Foreword

"Writing is not just career. You use writing to come to answers that will not come otherwise. Writing is the only way… it is the last resort of understanding your life, of cobbling your life together and, as the same time, giving it a frame that does not exist anywhere else". Thus begins novelist and literary critic Andre Aciman, while engaged in writing a book about his father... "the last few months of his life. He continues…were quite intense and I was very interested in capturing the end of a life from the perspectives of a son and from his own perspective, how did he register his life coming to an end…a life that has gone on for almost a century"!! According to him the most difficult part of life can be articulated more by writing than through any other method.

In the same vein Prof. Manu Kulkarni's insights on HELP (health, education, labour and pension) have been articulated upon through the written word in a manner no one else can capture such personal experiences of societal issues. With specific emphasis on how older people are perceived through several situational contexts, and what learnings are obtained for them is the subject matter for Manu Kulkarni. His background grounded in internationalism renders the writings a global appeal.

Prof. Kulkarni's retired status during the penning of these musings made his writing very relevant for our magazine called *Dignity Dialogue* on productive ageing and published by Dignity Foundation - an NGO committed to the cause of elderly in India. His articles invited a wide response from the readers who looked forward to the next instalment month after month. He became the recipient of Dignity Excellence Award in writing presented by Dr. Subir Gokarn, Deputy Governor of Reserve Bank of India on October 9, 2011 in Mumbai.

Development issues in this book are rendered as personal commentaries on the state of affairs. In the authors own words, 'they are the passionate outcomes of a development professional who has witnessed the development strategies around the world for more than four decades. They represent the views from the bottom of the pyramid where largest number of people survive'. My relationship with Prof. Manu Kulkarni commenced with his presentation of an outsider's view of the work we are putting in as a public trust. His perceptions of the role and responsibilities of organised NGOs and their contributions to society have lent very insightful understandings of the sector itself. When through his writing he became an insider, the manifold benefits we were reaching to senior citizen readers can be simply termed immeasurable.

It is an honour for me to be asked to write this Foreword to such high calibre 'musings' — an euphemistic term I should say to what really is an intellectual treatise. The sheer variety of development issues he addresses with critical insights in a simple, easy-to-understand prose, are a welcome addition to ethnographic literature in India.

24-09-2012 **Sheilu Sreenivasan**
Mumbai

Preface

This author has worked as a Development Professional over the years in several institutions such as the Indian Institute of Management, Ahmedabad, Administrative Staff College of India Hyderabad and UNICEF. Before joining these Institutes, the author also worked for a decade soon after his Post Graduation from the then Bombay School of Economics in 1964 in the Karnataka Administrative Service and gained insights on the problems of farmers, their land rights and farming and family disputes over land rights and how they survive and progress through conflict and compromise. The author had also a short stint in 1960 in the Agro-economic Research Centre established by the Ministry of Agriculture to do field research in the States of Gujarat and Rajasthan, which provided him the glimpses of rural life and living across the country. In UNICEF, this author had unique experience for nearly 20 years of observing the life and living of mothers, kids and their fathers behaviour, Bureaucrats and Politicians, Doctors and Midwives and Health care workers, school teachers to water engineers to sanitation experts to toilet cleaners in different parts of India and the world - from Afghanistan to Ghana to Nepal to the deserts of Rajasthan. This helped this author to gain enormous understanding of how the development programmes are designed at the top and how their benefits percolate down the line to the people at large, who are termed as beneficiaries in the bureaucratic language. Over the years, this author has also observed development programmes affecting people at large from watershed to social forestry to primary health care to microfinance enterprises to school education to urban and rural governance and the elderly people in their evening of their lives. This has enhanced this author's skills in observing how the programmes are designed by the Policy makers at the top and how they affect the people at large down the line.

These collection of articles - the short reflections on various dimensions of development -have been termed as Development Musings. The term "Muse" is derived from Greek Mythology in which nine Goddesses inspire anyone to write poetry or engage in creativity or gaze or ponder and reflect meditatively. In my case. I was inspired by many folks - and not Gods and Goddesses-such as editors, friends, professional colleagues and the most ordinary people who struggle to survive. The Founder of Dignity Foundation Dr. Sheilu Srinivasan in Mumbai was kind enough to provide space for my musings in their Monthly Journal "Dignity Dialogue". These Musings have appeared in this Journal for many years, and in this book they have been brought together for meditative reflections in a thematic manner by anyone interested in Development Issues. Development is a broad concept and can mean anything to anybody. But in this book, it is all about development of human beings, of the land and the mother earth and all about how we interact with each other and with physical environment, how the technologies affect humans from time to time and how development enhances human happiness or misery in different ways.

Health, Education, Labour and Pension (HELP) are the four biggest problems faced by the US citizens and also by many developing countries, and the Musings reflect how the old are being treated and how the growing 50+ age group people who are neither young or old are caught up between the shrinking job markets and the emerging talent shortage for new types of jobs. Parenting the Parents. The Global Paradox, Are seniors a Business Opportunity or a Liability ?, The Retirement Shock, Live Apart Couples - a Case of Emotional Disintegration, White-Black and Now the Red Market, Polio Eradication - the Untold Story in India, HIV/AIDS, Malaria and TB - the Diseases of the Civilization, Old-Older and the Oldest, When Doctors Differ you suffer, New Dimensions of American Elderly Care and many others — are a bunch of Musings, which capture the emerging trends of the aging population and the public health issues around the world and the choices available for the people to live well.

Another set of Musings - Generation X vs Generation Y, The Ernst and the Young Story, Corporate Social Responsibility - Myth or Reality ? Angry Youth and the Corrupt Old - brings into focus the need to bring in ethical values in governance at all levels. This is where the Leadership Pipeline from the bottom up in India assumes critical importance and the founders of India's freedom struggle such as Mahatma Gandhi and First Prime Minister of India Pandit Nehru were all leaders of high ethical values and were men of great intellectual eminence and studied in great Universities like Cambridge and London. Leadership Pipeline in India is most crucial for building India as a great and a complex nation with hundreds of languages and caste, creed and faiths. Where is my school? is a musing on how the kids are angry on the closure of schools in some States of India. Early childhood education is most critical for the growing kids who enter the world of jobs and adulthood.

Some Musings capture the environment issues around the globe from shrinking seals of capetown to barren hills of Alaska without snow and the Deva bhoomi - (Land of Gods) - the Uttarkhand in India where the land slides are a common site for the tourists and the pilgrims who visit the land of Gods and Goddesses. Environment protection has remained a slogan in many countries and Water Sanitation and Hygiene (WASH) is the biggest stumbling block for human well being in India. WASH is assuming as the biggest stumbling block for good health of poor Indians. Technologies are not tapped and the Bill Gates Foundation is spending billions of dollars to find out the best and the least cost toilets for the majority of the poor around the world. Will it help ?

Development Musings according to this author are ultimately the concerns of the people -children, adults, the young and the old and how they face the world full of chaos and diversity. Saints and spiritual Gurus, Yoga and Meditational experts have all played some role to bring peace of the mind to the people. Some musings on spiritual thoughts and deeds highlight the positive and negative roles of such spiritual icons in bringing peace to the young and the old. Teachings of a 12th Century Saint Basaweshwara is still relevant in the 21st Century - the teachings such as Work is Worship, Knowledge is power and many others. How these teachings can be spread without a tinge of any religious bias is the challenge before our saints and religious heads particularly in India.

Although these musings appear *prima facie* as disjointed, they still provide a glimpse of how the development programmes in different countries of the world affect the people in those countries from time to time and they also provide a glimpse into the politics and economics of development programmes from time to time. These musings are not research notes or reports based on micro and macro level statistical data analysis or Musings funded by Dignity Foundation to write for their monthly journal ! They are the passionate outcomes of a development professional who has witnessed the development strategies around the world for more than four decades. They represent the views from the bottom of the Pyramid where largest number of people survive and not the viewpoint of those at the top of the pyramid where the richest politicians and the corporate honchos decide the fate of the world economy. In the words of Mahatma Gandhi real development is all about the greatest good of the greatest number and not the greatest good of the *smallest number* who unfortunately decide the fate of the poorest and largest number of people in the world.

These development musings are also based on a wide variety of development reports, analysis by media celebrities, the websites and discussions with a wide variety of ordinary people around the world with whom the author had the privilege of talking over many decades. The author hopes the readers would muse over these development musings and enjoy them !

Acknowledgements

My Musings in the Dignity Dialogue published from Mumbai for several years have been a great inspiration for me to keep musing the development issues in the country and the world. My profound thanks are due to Dr Sheilu Srnivasan, the Founder of the Dignity Foundation who has inspired the ageing people in India to keep up their spirits high and to Shoba Nair, the Executive Editor of Dignity Dialogue for coaxing me to keep up the deadline of Manu's Musings Column and also enriching my Musings by her skillful editing.

As me and my wife Vijayalaxmi complete fifty years of our married life, this book is presented to her for completing the golden years of our enchanting life. We both hope our children Sanjay and his wife Renu and Shweta and her Husband Kirit get inspired by these musings and our grand children Aadi, Diya, Nachiket and Amogh, would glance these musings when they grow up.

1

The Changing Demography

Old, Older and the Oldest

On the state of the emerging elderly population in the country.

The recently concluded conference which this author attended at Chennai (March 25-27, 2010) on demographic dividend, population ageing and implications for health, organised by the International Institute for Population Sciences (IIPS) has thrown out many dimensions of caring for the elderly. As India moves to benefit from the demographic dividend, we will have a huge burden of caring for the old. Another conference that took place in February 9-11 at Trivandrum under the auspices of the Centre for Gerontological Studies (CGS), supported by the UN Fund for Population Activities, came out with a scary scenario on the state of the emerging elderly population in the country.

Now there are three internationally accepted classifications of the old — the young old (60-70 age group), the old old (70-80), and finally the oldest old (80+). Because of early demographic dividend in the Southern Indian States like Kerala, Tamil Nadu, and Karnataka, the speed of ageing is faster in these States. These States achieved low fertility rates, unlike UP and Bihar, in a span of 25 years and their older population is currently growing at an unprecedented annual rate of 3.5 per cent. Declining fertility and increasing longevity have resulted in an accelerated growth of the ageing population. Ageing is just not an economic and demographic issue, but a social, cultural and technological issue, and faces contentious problems related to healthcare costs, social support and financial security with major economic implications. The principles of older persons enacted by the UN in 1991 are independence, participation, care, self-fulfillment and dignity. But how to promote these is the real test of the Ageing Policy of the Indian Government.

Demographers are good in statistical analysis, but when it comes to policy prescriptions they flounder. They should know what all big and small agencies are doing (like Dignity Foundation, Mumbai, and its branches in major cities of India, Nightingale in Bangalore, etc.) to provide support and hand-holding to the ageing in our country. There are some policy controversies like increasing the age of retirement because of good health from 60 to 62. But what will happen to the large young, skilled population ready to get into jobs occupied by the older groups? Many States in India want to reduce the age of retirement from 60 to 58! The informal sector in India is huge and nobody retires there. The absence of a comprehensive coverage of Social Security is a major challenge in India.

The oldest (80+) are the hardest to manage because of health, emotional stress, support and care issues. Despite broken and globalised families, culturally they don't wish to depend on their children. The CGS suggests setting up three agencies to care and support this group — Multiservice Elder Care Centres, Senior Citizens' Clubs, and Geriatric Mobile Medicare Unit (GMMU).

Most of the oldest group (about 20 per cent) do have problems performing the Activities of Daily Living (ADL); another 30 per cent will be home-bound and a yet 30 per cent suffer from dementia. Most diseases of the oldest often have no cure and are called 'terminal diseases' in medical parlance. The women in this group have a different set of problems. Since women live longer than men, the extended period of life is spent more or less in morbidity and generally in widowhood and they need better support system and healthcare.

What is the cost involved in managing the lives of these different age groups of the elderly population in India is yet to be known since no research has ever been carried out.

The simplistic solution suggested by many is to increase the pension of the 80+ group. But that will not solve their problems. The policy initiatives from the Centre and the States so far are in the nature of hit and run tokenism. Even the definition of a Senior Citizen differs from department to department. In Karnataka, the State Transport buses provide concessions to the 60+ only in normal buses; in AC Coaches they are charged full rates! The Vishwesharaiah Technological University in Karnataka does not recognise a distinguished 70 year old Professor to guide Ph.D students. Like these, if we go on examining the elder-people friendly polices of the States or the Centre, we get depressing results!

We need many action agencies across the country to invest in the care of these delicate 80+ group. We have many care agencies such as Narayana Hrudayalaya, Shankar Netralaya, and Nightingale Home Health Services in Bengaluru who have done outstanding work in providing healthcare. The governments must now act to scale those services to cover the growing number of elderly citizens.

New Dimensions of American Elderly Care

Caring for an ageing parent, elderly spouse, domestic partner or close friend, presents difficult challenges - specially when a crisis hits and you are suddenly faced with the responsibilities of elder care. Caregiving can also begin as a result of a series of unsettling mishaps and warning signs that indicate a need for long term care.

As I sip my morning lemon tea in the swimming pool lawn of my son's residence in the Emily Street of Far Hills in NJ in the US, I was excited to read a lead article on 'Love and Commitment' in the New York Times Magazine of 23rd June, narrating the experience of the author, Jeneen Interlandi, on how she managed her 69 year old father suffering from bipolar disorder. I had heard only about Dementia and Alzheimer's as problems of the elderly. Now this chilling article explains the nature of bipolar disorder and how to manage the elderly people suffering from this dangerous disease. The symptoms are scary.

This author says her father, in the early December 2010, suddenly became paranoid and said some people were trying to kill him and he became violent and threatened to commit suicide. At one point he was trying to jump from the car when his wife was driving it, and on another day he poured motor oil on the windshield when his wife was taking out the car from, the garage, and more than once he hit his wife and threatened to burn the house down. Sometimes he would cry and apologise. He didn't know what was happening to him. The City Police had visited his house, but they could do nothing.

Skilled vs Social Care

Such behaviours are dangerous not just to the family but also to the neighbourhood, and the US City Government is caught between these dimensions - the caretaker and the State. When and how will such elderly persons be taken to the Psychiatric Emergency Screening Services (PESS), and put in Mental

Hospitals, has to be decided by the caretaker. As per the current practices, only people who posed an imminent danger to themselves are taken to the hospitals. The second is the Police — can they arrest persons with bipolar disorder for creating violence in the neighbourhood? Can such an old man or woman, who has nobody to look after, and loiter around the street and die, be arrested by the Police and put in jail? These issues are critical but there are no easy answers.

This particular person was admitted in a mental hospital and was released, and the question is how long can such a bipolar elderly person manage himself or herself? In the US everything is law, human rights protection and damages, and what have you. Some NGOs in the business of elderly care are pleading for human-friendly laws. Patient rights group say that any form of involuntary treatment - even outpatient treatment - would violate civil liberties and is tantamount to the forcible medication of the mentally ill. In each State in the US, there are separate laws for bipolar patients and are framed in memory of those who lost their lives because of schizophrenia. New York has Kendra's Law, named after a young woman pushed in front of a train by a man with schizophrenia, who had been turned away from several psychiatric hospitals. But a large number of mentally ill patients are not violent.

With such problems of the elderly emerging in this country, the care and support needed is vanishing because the young are busy with their jobs and careers, and the medical care is getting complicated as one can see from the reports emerging on the Medicare and the Medicaid and health insurance problems the Americans are facing. As reported in the *New York Times*, according to Medical Billing Advocate Jena Poole, who is helping patients in their Medical bills settlement, some clients are billed $11,000 for even a minute hand surgery.

There is a tacit understanding between the Insurance companies and the hospitals to inflate the cost and bill the patients. The uninsured have no bargaining power, so they are to pay much more, to health insurance experts in the US, it is narrated that "if you line up five patients in their beds and they all have their gall bladders removed and they get the exact medicine and service, if they have insurance or no insurance, the hospital will get five different reimbursements and none of it is based on cost. The insurers negotiate a different rate and if you are uninsured or underinsured or out of network, you are asked to pay full fare"! This is America, the land of capitalism and democracy, and how the elderly will manage their health and living is a great question. Because of this health economics conundrum, the elderly are hit hard, and the biggest election issue at present is how to fix these health problems of the Americans.

Danger Signals

- ***Sudden weight loss*** could be an indication that the elderly person is simply not eating or not preparing foods.
- ***Failure to take medication or over-dosing*** may indicate confusion, forgetfulness, or a misunderstanding of the doctor's instructions.
- ***Burns or injury marks*** may indicate physical problems involving general weakness, forgetfulness, or a possible misuse of alcohol.
- ***Deterioration of personal habits*** such as infrequent bathing and shampooing, not shaving, or not wearing dentures could be the result of either mental or physical problems.
- ***Increased car accidents*** can indicate slowed reflexes, poor vision, physical weakness, or general inability to handle a Vehicle.

- *General forgetfulness* such as not paying bills, missing appointments, or consistently forgetting name, address, phone number, and meal times could be a signal.
- *Extreme suspiciousness* could indicate some thought disorder. Your parents thinking that their neighbours, friends, family, doctor, and lawyer are all conspiring against them would be an example. Intense ungrounded fears about dire consequences may be a danger signal.
- *A series of small fires* could be caused by dozing off, forgetting to turn off the stove or appliances, or carelessness with matches. They may indicate blackouts or dizzy spells.
- *Bizarre behaviour of any kind* could be a warning sign. This behaviour could be dressing in heavy gloves and overcoat in 90 degree weather or going outside without shoes when it's snowing. Watch for uncharacteristic actions or speech.
- *Disorientation of a consistent nature* may indicate a need for help. Examples include not knowing who one is, where one is, who the family is, or talking to people who are not there.

The Missing 'Patient' in the American Health Reforms

As one glances through the huge media coverage of health reforms in the US, one is amazed at the way heathcare issues are debated. The debate is more focussed on insurance, drugs, Medicare and Medicadid complexities, billing by the hospitals, use and misuse of medical technologies in scanning the patient ailments, and so on. There is very little discussion on the 'Patient' and 'Doctor', their relationships, and how they care with concern and compassion. Many public health experts and primary healthcare researchers are concerned more with the primary care of the vulnerable groups in the US than with the hospital care.

As per the Kaiser Family Foundation, the US is spending almost $2.6 trillion annually on healthcare. The US health indicators are among the worst in the high income countries. Since the 1960s, the US dropped from 12th to 46th in infant mortality rankings (below Cuba and Slovenia), and from 16th to 36th in life expectancy (below Cyprus and Chile). In certain neighbourhood communities like Baltimore, Chicago and Los Angeles, the life expectancy for subsets of the population is lower than in Bangladesh.

Writing in the Stanford Social Innovation Review (Volume 10, Summer 2012) Rebecca Onie, Paul Farmer, and Heidi Behforouz-health experts from the Harvard Medical School - said, "The misalignment between the expansive goal of 'health' and the cramped definition of 'care' has cost the US untold lives and treasure. Yet realignment is in reach, through expanding the scope of the healthcare, the place where it is delivered, and the workforce that provides it. Thus the US healthcare system could significantly improve health outcomes and reduce the inefficiencies." In the 60s, half the Doctors in the US worked in Primary Care, but today barely 30 per cent do. Expanded insurance coverage will increase the number of patients seeking care, but from the same number of physicians. With 21 million potential Medicaid patients expected to enter the healthcare system in 2014, primary care physicians will face a double burden because of too many needing care, particularly the elderly and the poor.

Access to Good Healthcare

Good health at low cost was, and should be the dream of the poor and rich countries alike. But unfortunately the crony capitalism is showing is ugly face even in the field of healthcare in the US, having done enough damage in the field of banking and finance. In order to get good health, Four Ps are important-Patient, Place, Provider and the Product (service, drugs and outcomes). Except the first P all the remaining three Ps are in the limelight now. Recently, New York Times (July 12, 2012) reported about the price charged for drugs by doctors. When the Pharmacy sells a heartburn drug called *Zantac,* each pill will cost about 35 cents. But if a doctor dispenses it to a patient in their office or consulting room, they charge 10 times the original price i.e., $3.25 a pill!! Instead of sending patients to drugstore to get drug as per the prescription, the doctors dispense the drugs in their office or clinic, with the bills going to insurers. Thus the doctors can make tens of thousands of dollars operating their own in-office pharmacies.

In some hospitals, patients are flooded with several bills to pay. According to some Medical Bills Advocates, some patients are billed as much as $11,000 for even a minute hand surgery. There seems to be a tacit understanding between insurance companies and hospitals to inflate the cost and bill the patients! The insurers negotiate different rates, and if you are uninsured or under insured or out of network, you are asked to pay the full fare. The uninsured have no bargaining power, which is why they are expected to pay much more. What will happen to the poor families who cannot have two full meals and forget about health insurance? Where is the healthcare for them?

Doctors in big cities like New York are overloaded and they have no time to talk to patients to know their social needs like nutrition, early childhood care, etc., which are part of primary healthcare. According to the Health Leads Survey in the US, in some crowded hospitals in New York City, doctors spend hardly an average of two minutes per patient discussion. Medical care devices is another area with good business prospects, and in the name of Mobile health, devices like blood pressure cuffs and glucose monitors enable physicians and other care providers to check and treat patients' conditions without being physically present. By keeping patients out of hospitals, these medical devices may reduce cost and improve health. But the big. question is, if they fail to work, who will bear the-cost of a patients' life and death situation? The providers are also afraid of the repercussions that new medical technologies may cause to them and lead to many claims and damages. To conclude, on par with the capitalist slogan 'Customer is King', why not the US slogan for healthcare reforms read The Patient is King, and long live the Patient!'?

America is known for 'undocumented immigrants/citizens', who have no access for any kind of rights. Similarly, there are uninsured poor families who cannot be covered under Medicaid nor Medicare. For such patients, the way out is to build the primary care system. Many people don't know that Iran has the best healthcare for the rural poor. They have developed what are called 'Health Houses', which provide primary healthcare. These 17,000 Health Houses in Iran serve 23 million rural Iranians. Some US health experts in Mississippi are collaborating with the Iranian Primary Healthcare experts to establish such Health Houses to provide low cost healthcare to the blacks and others not covered by health insurance in the US.

Health Houses in Iran

Working in pairs out of modest, village-based facilities, the Islamic Republic of Iran's trained community health workers, the *Behvarzan,* from the Farsi words *beh* (good) and *varz* (skill), provide basic healthcare to most of the country's rural population. A female *behvarz* is responsible for, among other things, child and maternal health; a male *behvarz* for sanitation and environmental projects. Both workout of the Health House, a rural medical post and the most basic unit of service delivery in the country's healthcare plan.

"Health houses serve as the powerful arm of rural healthcare centres. They did well when the main issue in the country was to contain contagious diseases. They are doing the same now vis-a-vis chronic diseases like diabetes and hypertension, and also in improving nutrition, the control of iodine disorders, iron-deficiency anaemia, and fluoride treatment."

The health houses refer patients to rural health centres, which cover about 6000 to 10,000 people, and have up to two physicians and several health technicians. These centres are responsible for elective and emergency case management, supporting the health houses, and supervising both the health technicians and the *behvarzan.*

In Iran, preventive care is a priority and special attention is paid to high-risk groups such as mothers and children. Healthcare workers are chosen and trained within each community. Preventive and curative programmes are integrated seamlessly. The system is decentralised, which encourages regional facilities to become self-sufficient and empowers local communities. Iran's child mortality rate has dropped by 70 per cent since 1980, when the Health House concept was first implemented.

White, Black and Now Red !

Unlike black, white or gray markets, red markets exist in a different category because the product being traded cannot be valued in monetary terms alone. The value of human tissue is the value of life itself, and its costs are apin in blood.

Students of economics have been taught in their graduate days about market forces and how they operate in a typical country, and how citizens have to deal with them. We were told about perfect markets, imperfect markets, commodity and financial markets, and also about market collapse when demand and supply do not match and how the consumers behave in such situations. All this was a 'white market where everyone knew what is happening in the demand and supply of goods and services, and how the State regulates the market situation and also collects taxes from its citizens. When citizens started evading taxes and underhand dealings of bribery and corruption reached its height, the word 'black market' emerged. Now the black market is much stronger than white, according to many financial experts around the world.

Blood Money

Red Market: (noun) any economic system or economy that trades primarily in human parts or human beings.

Countries have now adopted the 'Red Market, which deals with the sale and purchase of all human organs, human foetuses, kidneys, human bones and what have you! The best source book on the red market is written by Scott Carney where he examines the features of this market, how it is emerging and how to regulate it - it at all it needs regulation (see 'box: Scott Carney, *The Red Market* Hachette Book Publishing India, 2011). From a single cell in the human egg to a fully grown child, everything is up for sale in the global red market. India is leading in the sale of all types of human organs including children in the name of adoption.

Despite the Human Organ Transplantation Act of 1994, the trade in human bones in Kolkata is a flourishing one. Instead of voluntar blood donation, now many hospital are doing a good business of bloo trade as well. Young poverty-stricken women sell their eggs for a price Unlike the blood donation which is not painful donating their eggs is painful process, and take a minimum of two weeks of hormone stimulation and then surgical removal.

Eggs of a woman fetch a high price compared the brown or a black women.

Who are all the brokers in this red market is a burning question. Unfortunately, some doctors and hospitals act like sharebrokers and stock exchanges, despite regulatory provisions to stop the sale of human organs like kidneys. Medical experts say that living donor transplants are more successful than cadaver donations, and patients who get kidneys from paid donors live longer than those who receive their organs from brain dead patients.

The tsunami hit coastline of Tamil Nadu, which Scott Carney visited, is a big centre in South India for kidney market and is termed the 'Kidneyvakkam' because, after the tsunami, fishing business lost its market and livelihood became difficult for these fisherfolks. In the US itself, there are more than 100,000 patients waiting for organ transplant and are surviving on dialysis, which is painful and costly.

Regulation or Removal?

It is shocking and inhuman that so many women, for want of livelihood opportunities, are selling their organs for survival, just as women sell their jewellery in times of financial difficulties. As the black market in money/currency transactions is regulated by agencies like SEBI, the red market in human organs has to be regulated by ethical doctors and transparent hospitals. Since only hospitals can perform the operations, it should be easy to regulate the red market transactions in India. This cannot be done without ethical practices by nurses, doctors and also by patients, in Shimoga, Karnataka, almost 40 human foetuses were dumped in the garbage near a Nursing Home, and among them 24 were of girls! Who will regulate this at the end of the day?

Sex determination tests of a baby in a mother's womb have now emerged as a flourishing trade despite the ban on such tests. There are boards put up by gynecologists in Punjab and Haryana: 'Beta or Beti-you can get here!' Baby girls are now in short supply. 'Better Rs. 500 now than Rs. 5000 later' reads one ad in a clinic in UP stressing the price of a sex test compared to a bride price! The red market is located at the complex interface of cultural attitudes, patriarchal prejudice, socio-economic pressures and misuse of modern medical technology. We need a lot of courage to kill this market.

The Red Market: Scott Carney

This is an in-depth report that takes readers on a shocking tour through a macabre global underworld where organs, bones, and live people are bought and sold on the red market. Investigative journalist Scott Carney spent five years on the ground tracing the lucrative and deeply secretive trade in human bodies and body parts - a vast hidden economy known as the red market. From the horrifying to the ridiculous, he discovers its varied forms: an Indian village nicknamed *'Kidneyvakkam'* because most of its residents have sold their kidneys for cash; unscrupulous grave robbers who steal human bones from cemeteries, morgues, and funeral pyres for anatomical skeletons used in Western medical schools and labs; an ancient temple that makes money selling the hair of its devotees to wig makers in America - to the tune of $6 million annually.

The *Red Market* reveals the rise, fall, and resurgence of this multibillion-dollar underground trade through history, from early medical study and modern universities to poverty-ravaged Eurasian villages and high-tech Western labs; from body snatchers and surrogate mothers to skeleton dealers and the poor who sell body parts to survive. While local and international law enforcement have cracked down on the market, advances in science have increased the demand for human tissue - ligaments, kidneys, even rented space in women's wombs - leaving little room to consider the ethical dilemmas inherent in the flesh-and-blood trade. At turns tragic, voyeuristic, and thought-provoking, *The Red Market* is an eye-opening, surreal look at a little-known global industry.

When Doctors Differ, You Suffer

At long last the WHO has declared the Swine flu (H1N1) as pandemic after dithering for months and after 144 deaths in 74 countries. But there was a wide spectrum, of divergent views and opinions on whether it is an epidemic or a pandemic or an endemic. This leads to the confusion on the part of the public agencies in different countries to get confused and postpone the much needed planning to tackle the pandemic.

The World's authority on public health - the World Health Organisation (WHO) - could not give its authentic and affirmative judgement whether by now Swine Flu is endemic or pandemic or an epidemic. The WHO Asst Director General, Dr. Keiji Fukuda, an authority on Influenza, has reluctantly admitted that "The WHO is preparing to declare the first flu pandemic in 40 years as a new H1N1 influenza strain that continue spreading throughout Latin America, Europe and now Australia." Dr. David Morens, an epidemiologist of the National Institute of Allergy and Infectious Diseases in the US says, "There is a lot of misinformation in the medical literature, and it is really quite hard to figure out what is and what is not a pandemic." Dr. Lawrence K Altman, another medical expert, writing in *The New York Times* under his 'Doctor's World' column says: "Scientists don't know precisely how pandemics arise, what fuels them, why they vary in their lethality, why some occur in waves and why they stop. Scientists like to assert theirs is an exact discipline. But the term pandemic turns out to be another example of imprecise vocabulary that doctors use everyday, assuming everyone understands their meaning. Journals, textbooks and reference works use pandemic in discussing certain diseases, but rarely define the word."

A 'Pandemic' Confusion

In the field of public health, many do not agree on the disease profiles in any given country. Although 'pandemics' generally cover infectious diseases, the term has spread to non-infectious, chronic ones like the pandemic of heart disease and obesity. Students of public health know of HIV/AIDS pandemic, cholera and dengue. Some experts think AIDS pandemic is only confined to Africa, although more people have died of HIV/AIDS in Asia and the other countries of the world. Many of the epidemics don't wait for the conclusive epidemiological evidence to emerge in any given country and given the sanitation problems of many countries like India, public health authorities have to be prepared for the worst scenario.

The WHO has an elaborate staging system to declare any disease as 'pandemic', but it has to be simplified and made understood by the Government public health agencies in a typical country like India, where Health Ministers of different States have to take fast decisions. Why should WHO wait for six stages to decide, after a toll of precious human lives? If we have to face this pandemic, institutes like the All India Institute of Hygiene and Public Health, Kolkata, has to engage in media campaign in different States to educate the lay public on do's and don'ts for facing such pandemic. This Institute has a poor track record on mass media education on such pandemics. Like the Centre for Disease Control in the US which educates the public through media campaigns like "Cold or Flu, Antibiotics Don't Work for you", our Institute has to become proactive to educate the public.

Parenting Your Parent: The Global Parandox

As I sip my morning tea in the green lawns of my son's house in New Jersey, the *New York Times* headlines, on the care of the elderly in the context of the painful US recession, catch my attention. Jobs are at a premium and the existing jobs are vanishing. What will happen to those elderly, depending on their sons, daughters and siblings? Caring is a trait more pronounced among the women than the men, not only among the Asian families but also among Americans. The recession in the US has placed special stress on the estimated 44 million Americans who provide care for an elderly or a disabled relative or spouse.

Role Reversal

In the survey carried out among 1005 caregivers by the National Alliance for Caregiving and Ever Care - a Division of the United Health Group - one in six said that they had lost a job during the downturn. Teresa Denk, 59, lives with her father, a former mechanic who is 92 and requires constant care. Denk has not held a fulltime job since 2000 when her mother developed cancer and required her daughter's fulltime care. Denk lives in Rainbow City in Atlanta and the recession has hit her badly. Earlier she worked as a pre-school teacher, did some medical coding work and worked in Wall Mart. She has never worked for nine years anywhere to get her Social Security benefit. If she starts collecting benefits at age 62, she will get about $450 a month, not enough even to pay the $520 rent on the apartment she shares with her father.

Two sisters, Marian and Carol who are above 56, look after their parents, and both are jobless at present. For people who quit their jobs to take care of their parents, there is no stimulus plan. Marian wants to write books and make money, but there is no cash to buy a computer and leaving their parents alone is uncomfortable. What to do? They are also worried about their own health in addition to the health of their parents. Care of the elders is a fulltime task that often precludes making money. This is the crux of the situation.

Who is Caring for the Caregiver?

Like Denk, Marian and Carol, there are hundreds of women across the US in a similar situation. As we think more deeply about their caregiving processes to their dependent kith and kin, it becomes scarier. Hundreds of self-employed, self-reliant, self-branded youngsters in the US are losing their income-earning capacity because of recession.

It is now called the 'self-employed depression', according to Emily Bazelon, the Truman Capote Fellow at Yale Law School in the US. When there is self-employed depression, the elderly dependants of these self-employed are also going to be under depression, perhaps leading to quicker mortality of the dependent elderly?

Caregiving is just not economics, but also involves culture, emotion, empathy and human touch. When one is young and has lots of money in the pocket, the conversation centres on investments, real estate, education of the kids and so on, and not on caring of their elderly dependants. There are stories about the eldercare, both good and bad, in India and elsewhere in the US. Culturally Indians are supposed to follow *pitru and matru devo bhava,* but in the recession both *Pitru* and *Matru* will have nuisance value. This is where the parental upbringing of the young becomes crucial and important. It is just not money which makes possible the caregiving, but it is the passion for caring the old and the infirm that drives the impulse to care.

Live Apart Together (LAT) Couples

Case of Emotional Disintegration

Marriage as an institution is now becoming outdated and in

the West it's all about "live apart together"(LAT) phenomenon. A new breed of LAT couples are emerging and in Britain the marriage rate (the per cent of married people per 1000 of population) dropped from 12.0 in 1991 to 9.2 in 2005 according to the office of National statistics in the UK . In several western countries including Europe, the fastest growing lifestyle is LAT. (See for an interesting analysis of LAT, Mark J Penn and E. Kinney Zalesne's "Micro Trends : Surprising Tales of the way we live today", Penguin, 2007). In Great Britain, it's 1 million couples - 3 in every 20 people aged 16-59 — which means many committed long term couples who don't live together as husband and wife. LAT couples are the newest players in the ever shifting panorama of today's family life.

Dual Dwelling Duos

Why is it happening in the West and will we in India also have LAT couples? It has serious implications for both young and old in India. Is it all about individual freedom of the married couple which leads to this phenomenon of LAT or is it all about economics of the working couple who want to live separately but visit each other occasionally? Is it all about breakdown in the emotional stability of couples or is it all about not caring and sharing or caring and sharing on-line? I am not a Sociologist or a counselor in family affairs, but as an elderly couple, my wife and I just imagined ourselves as LAT for some hours and felt it is horrible to be LATs!

As an economist I feel that LAT phenomenon may help the inheritance problems of the elderly and by being LAT they can always tell their kids that as husband and wife we are LATS and after our death no one will inherit their assets because they are not leaving anything for them to inherit. Western couples always share the kitchen work unlike Indian elderly husbands who never lift their plates and keep them in the dishwasher/sink, nor they share any household work Western wives are more individualistic than the eastern wives. Perhaps this has made them become LATs. How can LAT promote life-long relationships? Solo living has its own problems and the western wives are happy to discard the ailing husband or the husband can discard the ailing wife. Both situations are possible.

The biggest problem of LAT phenomenon is its effect on the children, particularly the growing adolescent ones. LAT couples are as good as divorcee concles trying to say 'hello' to their gives when they pass through the restaurants or shopping malls, No one has analysed their emotionally traumatised children. Julie EVONS has analysed the situation of children from broken homes who are always more distressed than their parents realise. (Ses Julie Lynn Evans' 'What about the children? How to help children. survive separation and divorce", Bantam Press, 2008} They are generally rude clings deductive or attention-seeking. If one of the parents poisens the child's mind, it is as good as steeling the childs natural, physical emotions and spiritual inheritance. LAT couples are as good as separated and the effect of LAT phenomenon needs to be researched by sociologists, family counseling experts and those who speak for the wellbeing of children and kids.

Retirement Shock

Does retirement necessarily means disillusionment, slow decline in intellect, and loss of social respect?

I started working at age 26. In my long career, I have worked for a State Government, a premier Indian Institute of Management, Administrative Staff College of India, Hyderabad and finally the UNICEF from which I retired after 20 years of service at age 60 in 1998. Most of us in India retire either at 58 or at 60 and nowadays many retire prematurely and some retire voluntarily. Post retirement, an important concern is how to live with dignity. The word dignity is open to interpretations. But there are certain commonly accepted principles of dignified living like not being dependent on others in old age, ability to live, within one's means, enjoying fairly good health, trying to be helpful to others, sharing one's own experience and wisdom for the good of society and the unfortunate, etc. With better health, more people are going to live longer and therefore the concept of dignfied living becomes even more crucial. One of the biggest problems faced by many employees is absence of retirement planning. Years ago L and T used to run a programme for their employees called planning for retirement. This is very much required today, particularly in our big cities like Mumbai, Bangalore and Kolkata, where thousands retire every year. Bangalore alone has some 8,000 highly paid retired officers whose knowledge and experience is not used by any agency or government.

Retirement is threatening for many officers, particularly those who enjoy a lot of power and privileges and not necessarily wealth. While in office, they have orderlies. *chaprasis,* big bungalows, many drivers and a whole retinue of hangers-on. One fine day, when they retire, all these vanish. Some get heart attacks and even succumb! But those who enjoy all these perquisites never plan for their retired living. As a result, many suffer from mental shock on retirement. Some retirees face problems relating to children's education, housing, moving household stuff and pension. Many retirees never plan their investments, debt payments, etc.

Most fear retirement. Some make hurried plans to perform the marriages of their daughters before retirement. Some officers keep their retirement date secret lest subordinates stop respecting them! A colleague in UNICEF had asked me to not divulge his retirement date to anybody in government lest they stopped respecting him.

Post retirement, some jump into politics and contest elections and try to become ministers. I have seen some senior bureaucrats who have become ministers after retirement face cultural shock as people - any voter who claims he/she has voted for him - take the liberty to meet them anytime anywhere, anyhow, which they find annoying. These are often miserable and 'decline' both in the eyes of the voters and in their own self esteem!

After retirement, some end up as freelance consultants. But these are the days of 'domain knowledge' and 'niche' areas. A generalist administrator has no place in this fast moving new economy. Very few can set up big ventures after retirement. Many piggyback on some institutions or use their old 'contacts' to do consultancy or take up salaried jobs. All these arrangements work out well for some time but even if health permits, one cannot work 9 to 5 after 65-70.

Another aspect of a retiree's life is the 'space' and 'time' occupied by him or her in a family. Dependence leads to decline. Today technologies have reduced the dependence of the aged on human hands. 90 per cent of the aged in the US are dependent on Internet which gives them enormous freedom to talk and chit chat. Given our state of technologies, retirees in India have to pick up the rudiments of digital literacy. And the results are rewarding. My elderly friend aged 75 who retired as Chief Justice of a state High Court and has two children settled abroad recently installed a computer at his place and got Internet connection. Now he is all the time in front of the small screen browsing world news and chatting with his children and grandchildren. Becoming techies as we get older is one way of remaining young.

In the US, where 35 million people are above 65 and make up 13 per cent of the population, the word 'dependence' has now been replaced by the word 'assisted.' My wife and I visited a posh old age home called a Centre of Assisted Living in West Orange in New Jersey. To walk through its living space was a revelation. Even if something untoward happened to an inmate in the toilet, an alarm would go off in the reception and within seconds the victim would be assisted.

Unfortunately, the concept of 'assisted living' has not caught the planners of old age homes in India. Some of the old age homes run and managed by erstwhile Gandhian and Saryodaya-workers are in a total mess because they have not changed with the times. You cannot force retirees who opt to be in such old age homes to get up early, pray and spin and wear khadi clothes. The majority of the old age homes in India, meant for middle income and lower income retirees, are like prison houses. They are run by well-intentioned people, but good intentions are no excuse for incompetence as says Peter Drucker. management guru of this century. We have to run them professionally and we have to combine compassion with competence.

Japan, a nation of old people, can show us the way. At one time, Japan had crude traditions like *Uba* Sute (literally throwing away the old women off to the mountain side once their spouses died to save the cost of feeding them!). Now, we can learn from them how to run old age homes. Yo Hatakeyama, Manager of the Fukueikai Home for Older people in Tokyo's Shinagawa ward says, "Do not take too much care, better if old people did more for themselves." Do not stay in bed is the first rule in their old age home.

Our old ways of caring have to give way to new and better ways, which are cost effective. It is not medical technology which alone can give us better options. It is finally the human touch and care which enable us to live with dignity.

Sewa Dham Ashram

A Rainbow of Compassion and Care

This non-government, voluntary organisation is like a hermitage set in natural surroundings that takes care of the downtrodden with a missionary zeal.

Service is a journey into Darkness
Enlightening Earthen Lamp
every step Lamenting the Loss of Flame
is no excuse Be Flame yourself and burn ...

— *Sudhirbhai Goel, Founder and Chief Trustee, Sewa Dham Ashram*

These words sum up the spirit and passion of Sudhirbhai's work in Sewa Dham Ashram near Ujjain, where service, compassion and care take centrestage. At the age of 16, Sudhirbhai, wanting to be a Doctor, went to meet Gandhian Dr. Susheela Nayyar in Wardha. But instead of enrolling in a Medical College he stayed back in the Vinoba Bhave Ashram in Wardha. At the time Vinobaji was in *mounvrat,* and he gave a chit asking Sudhirbhai why he wanted to meet him. Sudhirbhai said he wanted to serve as a doctor. Vinobaji informed he could serve the poor without being a doctor! So he came back to Ujjain to start a shelter for lepers. Once Mother Teresa was visiting Ujjain and Sudhirbhai requested the Bishop to arrange her visit to his shelter for the Lepers. The Bishop refused, but undaunted Sudhirbhai's group waited on the road through which Mother was to pass. Getting down from her car, Mother spent one hour with them and inspired him to continue his work. That was the turning point in Sudhirbhai's life. He motivated the lepers to shun begging and organised training workshops in various trades. He constructed a community hall and strove to rehabilitate the cured ones in the mainstream of society. Marriages were also performed in this colony.

Now at 49, he's passionate about Sewa Dham Ashram (SDA). Founded 17 years ago, the Ashram is situated in a picturesque location 20 km from Ujjain, adjoining the Gambhir Dam in 17 *bighas* of land. It's a beacon of hope for about 240 mentally-retarded, HIV-affected, parents discarded by wealthy kids almost like "disposable clothes", earthquake victims, orphaned children and the old and the infirm. Ujjain is a pilgrimage for the old and disabled who come to seek blessings of Lord Mahakal after a dip in the River Chapra. Sudhirbhai narrates with emotion how some parents are escorted by their children who promise to be back by the time they finish their holy dip, but never return. Left in the lurch, many turn to Sudhirbhai's Ashram.

No one is denied entry on grounds of sex, religion, caste and creed or region. Just as you walk into the dilapidated huts of the Ahsram, you hear Ram Ramji and Sat Sri Akalji and Khuda Haifz - hundreds of feeble voices from India. Sudhirbhai reels out the stories of every Inmate of the Ashram. The stories of some are poignant and shocking. Jeevatiben who worked with Mahatma Gandhi as a child in Porbander, has been in SDA since the last five years. Now 100 years old, she's still alert and narrates Gandhiji's exploits and says she feels "young" in SDA. Raj Kumari Awasthi (80) has donated her entire property worth Rs. 15 Lakhs to SDA because she was cheated by her kith and kin. She was married at 15 into an orthodox brahmin family, but became widow just after six months. She managed to secure a degree and entered the Ujjian Education Department and retired after four decades, taking care of her in-laws all the while. When they disowned her after all this, she came to SDA in agony and is now a part of Sudhirbhai's mission.

Facilities

The inmates are looked after round-the clock, with utmost

care and love by male and female staff and professional attention by qualified physicians. They're provided with cot with bed and mosquito net, clean clothes, tooth paste, hair oil, comb, towel, all utensils for tea, breakfast, lunch and dinner - everything personal for each inmate along with musical instruments and TV for entertainment. Since its inception 14 years ago, the Ashram has sheltered 1094 inmates. Those who crave for reunion with their families are motivated and supported to do so. Around 398 inmates have returned to their families.

Sevanjali

After the untimely death of his only son Ankit at the tender age of 8, Sudhirbhai was eager to do something for special children. So he started *Sevanjali,* a school for deaf and dumb children at Ujjain in 1993. Specially trained teachers are appointed to teach these children. The school runs regular classes from KG to Class XII. Besides teaching, students are also trained in pantomime, dancing, handicrafts, drawing and painting, gardening, etc. to help them participate in state-organised festivals.

Sudhirbhai also started Bai Shramik Vidyapeeth (under National Child Labour Project) for the benefit of child labourers who're forced to work for their livelihood, He opened a school for them to continue studies along with their work. Classes are run on regular basis along with vocational training.

Shaken by the havoc created by the earthquake in Gujarat, Sudhirbhai went to Gujarat with 25 volunteers. He worked for 13 months in Kutch, Bhuj and Anjar with support from Blind Peoples Association, Ahmedabad and other organisations from Indore, Pune, Anjar, New Delhi etc.

Sahayata Centre

The Centre benefits the poor and needy patients in the premises of Ujjain Civil Hospital by distributing medicines, clothes and other necessary items. Also, it facilitates X-rays, CT Scan, Sonography etc. on a concessional rate from outside. It conducts multifarious social activities like organising free eye camps, polio drive and health camps for the needy with various kinds of reproductive health and family planning programmes, not only at Ujjain but in entire Malwa Region of Madhya Pradesh, specially in the tribal areas of Ujjain, Dewas, Jhabua and Shajapur.

Ten-in-One

Today Sewadham Ashram is Ten-in-one. It has an Old Age Home, Rehabilitation Centre, Desolate Women Abode for the exploited, Home for those with Down-syndrome, Orphanage homeless children, Special Care Centre for AIDS patients, Maharshi Dayanand Vanvasi Vidyapeeth for tribal children, Asylum for Lepers, Mercy Home for those on deathbed, and a Gaushala for abandoned cows.

Eye and Body Donation

Funerals are arranged with full rites for the dead inmates as per Hindu shastra, Bohra, Muslim, and Christian scriptures. Inspired by Baba Amte's 'life after death' concept, dead bodies are disposed through burial *(Samadhi)* and trees are planted at the spot. Sevadham has donated 76 pairs of eyes to Lions Club and Amar Jyoti, Netra Kosh, Ujjain so far. It has also donated bodies to R D Gardi Medical College, Ujjain, Mahatma Gandhi Medical College, Indore and Aurveda College, Ujjain.

Funding

Sudhirbahi thanks the Jain Saints who visit his Ashram from time to time for publicising his work around the country. Didwania Ratanlal Trust of Mumbai donates Rs. 30,000 every month to meet the cost of the institution. Then there are innumerable entreprenuers from Indore, Ujjain, Mumbai, Delhi and Kolkata whose contributions keep SDA going. And contrary to the normal principle of "pay and stay", SDA believes in "Just stay happy and die in grace".

Saving Lives : Good Politics and Economics

The National Rural Health Mission (NRHM) in India, 2005-2012, was launched to revitalise a crumbling public healthcare system. A cornerstone of the reforms was the introduction of a cadre of women from villages/hamlets called Accredited Social Health Activists (ASHA).

India's infant mortality rates in the early 80s were on par with the African countries, and despite many efforts of the Ministry of Health and Child Welfare, mothers in the rural areas could not deliver safely, and tetanus infection was rampant. The BMRU states of Bihar, MR Rajasthan and UP were dubbed as "Bimaru" regions for their high rates of infant mortality ranging from 120 to 130 per 1,000 live births. In our yearly ritual of observing and praising high-flying society women in the International Year of Women, we forget to compliment and reward the unknown women across the country who have pioneered "Saving Lives" of the newborn and their mothers.

In the words of late James Grant, Head of UNICEF from 1979 to 1998 saving lives is good politics and good economics. When more babies die, more babies are wanted by the mothers and the vicious circle goes on. We can stop newborns from dying with preventive steps like safe deliveries by observing some simple Cs - clean handling by the traditional birth assistants, clean place, and clean umbilical cord cutting. Once the mothers are assured of their babies' births and survival tor the first year, they would opt for no more kids. With fewer kids, there would be less expenses for childcare and more disposable income. This simple economics was not understood by late Sanjay Gandhi who enforced family planning in the 80s Even now, our politicians don't understand this good politics behind saving lives.

Now it is indeed heartening to read a report by *Down to Earth* on how ordinary village women are helping mothers in BMRU States to save their newborns. *Mitanins* and ASHAs in Chhattisgarh are now the most respected health workers, more than the doctors in government hospitals, because they are the ones who persuade pregnant mothers to deliver in hospitals than at homes. But they are just paid Rs. 250 as transport allowances. In the recent UP elections, misuse of National Rural Health Mission funds to the tune of hundreds of crores of rupees was reported. But this misuse is at the top level, from the doctors right up to the Health Minister and his bureaucrats. But in the Hamirpur district of UP, a traditional birth attendant *(dai)* called Ramkali has saved many mothers and their newborns by promoting hospital deliveries, although many *dais* insist on home deliveries because they are used to it for generations. Even in the difficult hill regions of Uttarakhand, ASHAs help the pregnant mothers deliver in hospitals.

Unsung Heroines

During my field travels in MP as a UNICEF professional in the 90s, many village mothers used to describe Auxiliary Nurse Midwives (ANMs) as 'Aati Nahi Midwives'. Being government functionaries, they were not bothered about visiting villages to carry out antenatal care of pregnant mothers and malnourished children in the *Anganwadis.* The ANMs claimed false travel allowances and cheated the health department and village mothers.

Thanks to the media and the grassroots leadership of village women like ASHAs and *Mitanins* in these BMRU States, mothers have been empowered and the lives of newborns have been saved. The credit must go to these passionate women who have shown leadership qualities, not to the doctors who shun village visits all the time.

In the Kota district of Rajasthan, 80 per cent of the posts of doctors are lying vacant, but still the ASHA *sahayoginis* - as they are called in Rajasthan - have made a difference to the lives of mothers and are now capable of checking blood pressure to haemoglobin!

We are honouring society women who have made some contribution to urban middleclass habitats, but none of the flagship organisations in the country is honouring these unseen women who have saved thousands of lives of rural newborns. God bless them!

The Mitanin programme is a Community Health Worker (CHW) programme initiated by the Government of Chhattisgarh in 2002, and was a precursor to the ASHA programme launched by the Government's National Rural Health Mission (NRHM) in 2005. The objective of NRHM is to strengthen the healthcare delivery system, with a focus on the needs of poor and vulnerable sections among the rural population. One of the main tenets of the mission is to identify one ASHA per 1,000 population in the rural areas, with the purpose of supporting the community to access public health services. She is expected to create awareness on health and its determinants, mobilise the community towards local health planning, and increase utilisation of the existing health services.

Bitter, better or Bt brinjal?

A battle is raging over a vegetable that is crucial to nutritious diet

I am neither a scientist nor a shareholder in multinational company Monsanto or its Indian partner Mahyco. I am a proud grandson of a typical farmer of north Karnataka and my cousins are still engaged in farming. When the genetically modified

(GM) cotton known as 'Bt cotton' controversy started, I picked up my camera and went to talk to farmers who had been growing desi cotton like 'Laxmi' and 'Jayadhar' earlier but had switched to Bt cotton. I found that farmers growing the new variety are now getting a good price and their income from Bt cotton has gone up because the cost of pesticide spray has gone down.

Now the controversy is about Bt brinjal. The vegetable is widely consumed in India. There are hundreds of local varieties of brinjal grown across the country. According to activist group Annadana, Karnataka's .4,000-year-old Udupi Mattu Gulla faces grave threat of extinction if Bt brinjal is released. But farmers are growing such brinjal despite incurring huge pesticide costs.

According to Belgian molecular scientist Prof Marc Van Momtagu, founder of the Institute of Plant Biotechnology for Developing Countries, "Activists should really take a hard look at the ethics and morality of their untenable position. Potentially life-saving technologies such as bio-fortified staple crops are blocked from reaching the farmers as a result of safety concerns broadcast by a variety of organisations. Bt brinjal variety in India has been produced to provide resistance to an insect pest that ravages 5 lakh hectares of brinjal cultivated in India."

However, according to scientist Dr P M Bhargava appointed by the Supreme Court as observer on the Genetically Engineered Crop Approval Committee (GEAC), the present trials are not enough to pass judgment on the efficacy of Bt brinjal: at least eight years must pass before a verdict can be reached. Then why did the Indian government approve its release? Why are Monsanto / Mahyco in such a hurry to release the seeds?

Another funny aspect is that spiritual gurus like Sri Sri Ravi Shankar and Baba Ramdev have told disciples not to eat Bt brinjal. What is the logic in telling disciples not to eat GM vegetables, which are not *tamasic?* They are as *satvic* as any other vegetable.

Activists who are supposed to be representing the farmers of this country are up in arms against Monsanto/Mahyco who have been allowed by GEAC to bring this type of GM brinjal seed to be sown by the farmers. Crop scientists, the government, the activists opposing GM crops, seed selling companies like Mahyco are at loggerheads - and the poor Indian farmer is nowhere in the picture.

Some five years back, a similar controversy erupted in the country against Bt cotton and now in India 80 per cent of the cotton grown belongs to the Bt variety of cotton. Spreading misinformation is the biggest sin that can be committed by any scientist, spiritual guru or activist. Mahesh Bhatt, the producer, has made a film called *Poison on the Platter.* The film blatantly shows that in some areas in the country, farmers who plucked Bt cotton have been poisoned and some have died. This is totally false. I have seen many farmers growing Bt cotton enjoying plucking it.

Now we are getting GM tomato. It has a longer shelf life. Farmers and consumers will get the advantage of less wastage. Let us hope that we get the best food in the days to come.

Polio Eradication in India : Untold Story

Public health experts and those engaged in the Universal Immunisation Programme (UIP) since the 90's in India should feel happy about the reported zero incidence of Paralytic Polio in 2011. Unlike smallpox, polio cannot be eradicated only by vaccination, say some experts. The year 2000 was the target date set by the World Health Organisation for polio elimination, if not total eradication.

When the UIP was launched in India in 1979, it was a tough task and India had no cold chain system to preserve the heat sensitive vaccines in the length and breadth of the country. International agencies like the UNICEF played a pioneering role, thanks to the support of the then Prime Minister Indira Gandhi, in pushing this programme to protect the mothers and children of India. Unlike smallpox which was a debilitating killer, the diseases affecting newborn kids and their mothers are of a complex nature and involve a timespan of several months for complete immunisation without missing any one vaccine. Three doses of polio and DPT vaccination with a month's interval, one time BCG at birth and one dose of measles on the child's ninth month, two doses of Tetanus toxide for the pregnant mother - is not an easy schedule to stick to by the health workers or the mothers. Missed vaccines are almost like lost vaccine!

Millions of dollars were spent by the UNICEF between 1980 to 2000 in building the cold chain required to keep the vaccines potent from the manufacturing place to the arm and mouth of the mother and child across India. Four main partners were involved in the UIP programme-the State and the Central Health Ministries and their entire staff down the line, ending with the village/urban health worker, the cold chain infrastructure to keep the vaccine potent (Polio vaccine has to be kept all the time at +2 to +8 degree centigrade), and the pregnant mother willing to be vaccinated by tetanus toxide and also get her newborn vaccinated without missing any dose. Finally, the husbands who have to cooperate with their wives and kids to get all the doses completed, come what may!

Doctors and health specialists think vaccine-preventable diseases are easy to be eradicated once the vaccines are made available. Polio was discovered almost 100 years back; then how come it has taken so many years to eliminate it from the Mother Earth?

'Pulse Polio'

Public health is a management challenge, and modern methods of management were deployed in India in this massive UIP operation. One is the effective cold chain system for vaccine preservation and administration. Second was the 'social marketing of good health practices' to save the child and mother, third was Pulse Polio campaigns across the country, involving Chief Ministers of States to launch these flagship events.

When I was head of the UNICEF in Haryana in the 80s, late Devi Lal was the Chief Minister, and my team invited him to put the polio drop to a smart kid to launch the Pulse Polio programme. Devi Lalji didn't know where to put the drop and in his Haryanvi style he asked the kid, *"Beta, ankh kholo* (Son, open your eye)". I had to intervene quickly to tell him to put the polio drop in the mouth, and not in the eye! In those days, Devi Lalji was suffering from eye ailments and he thought all drops were to be put in the eye! But he was a great leader and had an open mind to learn and personally monitored the UIP in Haryana, so there were few vaccine related deaths in Haryana in those days.

The Pulse Polio events or the Mass Immunisation Campaigns were our Parliament and Assembly elections, and any comparison between polling and vaccination may appear absurd! But think again. Elections are the only events well conducted in India - every step from voters' list to the voting, the counting, and to the declaration of the results, are perfectly managed. The mass immunisation camps in India in the 90s were managed like the polls -first is the enumeration of the eligible infants and pregnant mothers for vaccination. Just as all members in a family cannot vote, similarly not all can be vaccinated! Only infants and pregnant mothers had to be vaccinated/immunised. Enumeration of infants and mothers had to be done in rural and urban areas just like voters' list preparation. Unlike voters who can vote till they die, vaccination cannot be done to old people. After voting, the voter gets an indelible mark on his index finger as proof. Similarly, if the infant is vaccinated with BCG, there will be a scar on its arm!

These Pulse Polio events were the great experiments in public health across the world, where the Lions Club Members, Rotarians, and many activist groups played a great role not just in providing global funds for polio eradication, but also time and field- level campaigns and mobilisation of mothers and kids.

But this untold story is forgotten, and as India celebrates the success of Polio eradication, some public health activists now hint that polio eradication is a dubious claim (see Anant Phadke, *The Business Line,* 27 Jan 2012). According to some cynics, Oral Polio Vaccine (OPV) causes Vaccine Associated Paralytic Polio (VAPP) in a minuscule proportion of receivers - an average 1 case of VAPP per 4 million doses of Polio. But according to Dr Jacob John of Christian Medical College, Vellore, and a pioneer in Child Immunisation issues, to prevent VAPP we have to switch on to Inactivated Poliovirus Vaccine (IPV) and reach 90 per cent coverage, and then only stop OPV.

Only after we ensure the absence of wild and vaccine poliovirus can we claim complete success on polio eradication. According to a WHO spokesperson, "Continued high level vigilance for polio, emergency preparedness and intense immunisation activities will be essential for rapid detection of any circulating poliovirus". The virus is transmitted through contaminated food and water, and knowing the sanitation situation of our country, one wonders how the virus can be killed!

This is the great challenge now, and given the political will and the mothers' passion to protect their kids, it is not difficult to achieve 'Zero Polio' in the years to come and make our Indian kids smile and run, and not cry and limp.

Diseases of the Civilisation

There is an urgent need to eradicate the diseases of our civilisation, such as HIV/AIDS, malaria and TB.

Human health has remained mysterious despite great advances in medical research, diagnosis and drug discoveries. Currently, only the smallpox has been eradicated, and many diseases affecting kids like Polio and measles are still hovering despite huge resources spent on their eradication by nations and the UN Agencies like the UNICEF. According to the WHO, there is a difference between eradication and elimination - the former is total destruction of the disease from the humans, and the latter keeps appearing in some geographical pockets once in a while and has not been totally wiped out from human habitats. Only the smallpox has been eradicated in the world.

The HIV-AIDS, malaria and tuberculosis have remained as flagship diseases of the 21 st century. Some describe these as diseases of the civilisation because they reflect human greed, and unethical human behaviour! AIDS was first recognised in the 80s in the US, though it must have, been in existence much earlier. In India, even to talk about it was taboo, as it was shown to have emerged due to unprotected sex, prostitution and drug addiction: In South Africa, when hundreds were affected by AIDS, the then President Thabo Mbeki ridiculed the experts and dubbed it as a western disease and blocked all medical interventions. Hence South Africa suffered from AIDS in a big way. As a UNICEF Representative in Madhya Pradesh, I did a study in 1997 at the request of the MP Government, about the sexual behaviour of truckers and how they were being exposed to this dreaded disease, because they are away from their families for months together. Many laughed at this whole study as irrelevant. But when medical reports poured in from the numerous primary health centres of MP on the alarming incidence of AIDS among truckers, Ministers and MLAs got panicky, but still kept on denying the spread of this disease. The best defence practised by our politicians is denial!

According to the 2011 UNICEF Stocktaking Report on HIV/AIDS, in the Eastern Europe and Central As a 'Blame and Banishment' is fueling among a million young children was live and work on the streets. What is their future, no one knows! This culture of blame and banishment need to be replaced by care no compassion, suggests the UNICEF.

A Fight to the Finish

As we cross 2011, the world is still witnessing the continuance of these three diseases, but there is now a will by philanthropists such as Bill Gates and Warren Buffet to fight these diseases of the civilisation. The antiretroviral drugs are very expensive and on an average those affected have to spend as much as $ 5000 to10,000 per year. But the HIV vaccine is yet to be discovered, and many poor people who cannot afford the costly drugs still die, as in the African countries like Somalia and Congo. The most tragic situation is the HIV-affected pregnant mothers transmitting the virus to their newborns. It is found that a single dose of *Nevripine*-the antiretroviral drug - can halve the risk of the infected mother transmitting the virus to her child.

The elite section of society is more worried about cancer and lifestyle diseases than AIDS, TB and malaria, viewed as diseases of the poor. Big pharmas do more R & D on the drugs affecting the rich than the poor. The UN bodies like UNAIDS have no money to spend on these expensive antiretroviral drugs, and they go more for advocacy for interventions like male circumcision to stop the spread of HIV. But these are no substitutes for the urgent need for an HIV vaccine to control the disease. If these three diseases are to be eradicated, a strong alliance of science, activism and altruism should take place. These diseases of the

21st century need the highest level of altruism more than anything else, because altruistic motives alone can push the science and medical discoveries supported by philanthropists like Buffet and Gates. It is unfortunate that hardly any Indian philanthropist has come forward to fight these diseases of the century.

Japanese Burden, India's Dividend

Japan is heading Into a demographic vortex. It is the fastest ageing society on earth and the first big country in history to have started shrinking rapidly from natural causes.

Japan's median age (44) and life expectancy (83) are among the highest, and its birth rate (1.4 per woman) is among the lowest anywhere in the world, in the next 40 years its population, currently 127 million, is expected to fall by 38 million. By 2050, four out of ten Japanese will be over 65, so reports *The Economist* of London. It is called 'hyper ageing', and no other country has grown so old, so rapidly. Japan has some 40,000 bonafide centenarians, also described as pension parasites! Japanese governments have made efforts to encourage people to have more babies by enhancing child benefits and daycare centres in the last 30 years. Still, the birth rates are very low and the dearth of babies is now impacting the Japanese economy.

Weddings in Japan are very expensive, going up to $40,000! Six out of 10 women in their mid to late 20s — the best period for fertility — are still unmarried. When they get old, they live with their parents, living on their pensions and doing odd jobs. Quite a few are sent out of their homes. Many Japanese youngsters have watched their mothers divorce their fathers on retirement. Those men are cruelly termed as 'dead wet leaves', whose wives have trouble sweeping them out of home. The Japanese are also learning from personal experience that looking after elderly parents can be costlier and more time consuming than looking after children.

Land of Plenty

Look at India, a picture in the reverse. As a member of the National Population Commission (NPC), I am informed more about how the BMRU States are handling fertility control than mortality control, because these are the States where fertility is still high, although in the long run, control of mortality will bring down fertility You ask any mother, in the BMRU (Bihar, MR Rajasthan and UP) States, and she will state, "What to do? have more children, at least some will survive and many will die; that is why want more kids!" With better education of the mothers, more than the 'fathers, fertility can be brought down; and with better primary education, demography will also change for good.' India needs to stabilise her population, and we have a scheme called Janasankhya Stihartha Kosh-population stabilisation fund.

Naveen Jindal, the young dynamic member of the NPC and member of Lok Sabha from Haryana, says we have to address:

- the financial insecurity among the elderly
- stable and manageable population for the country
- and stabilise the population which is economical to the nation, on an opportunity cost principle (see his piece in *Economic Times,* January 2, 2011).

According to Jindal, it roughly costs Rs. 10 lakhs for a middleclass family to bring up a child till the age of 20, borne by the parents or the nation or the society. This amount is also the opportunity cost for the country as a whole for educating a child, taking care of its health, and so on. Three children mean Rs. 30 lakhs. If we persuade parents to have only one child, and tell them the balance Rs. 20 lakhs will be given to them separately if they agree for sterilisation or any other method of fertility control, it would save the country Rs. 20 lakhs, which can be given to parents in their old age for a dignified living. This amount can be invested in the joint name of those parents who have agreed to have a single child or two, depending on the situation and the health of the couple.

In the early days of Emergency, when Sanjay Gandhi piloted the sterilisation programme in India, it was misfired because the Government never did any homework as Jindal has done, and there was no incentive immediately or later for parents who opted for restricting the number of kids. Young men and women were forced to undergo sterilisation or tubectomy to achieve the targets fixed by the fearful health department functionaries.

What is not clear from Jindal's analysis is on the highly educated young married couples who need not be given incentives for undergoing vasectomy or tubectomy, since they already know the value of limiting the family size. The fund should be aimed, at the most poor and unorganised sectors, and not for the higher income group.

Help-in the United States of America

Health, Education, Labour and Pension (HELP) are the four biggest problems faced by the new President of the US. How he tackles these are going to determine whether he will be re-elected for a second term. All these cannot be left to the market forces, and the Bank scams in the US have shown that free market capitalism is not the answer for promoting good, health of the people, make them educated and provide jobs to the emerging talent in the country and take care of the old and ageing citizens.

The recession in the US is just not the problem of the young in search of shrinking jobs, but also a problem for the middle-aged folks in the 50's who are neither old nor young, but caught in the midst of shrinking job markets and the emerging talent shortage for new types of jobs. Re-training and re-skilling is now the mantra for those middle-aged who lose jobs. Tens of thousands of workers have been laid off in the automobile and manufacturing sectors. Mike Hutchins, 58, lost his $85,000 a year job in the automobile unit, where he worked for 25 years. He got re-trained as a computer-aided design engineer, but could not get any job even after attending a course in a Community college. Like him, there are many who are getting re-trained but cannot get a job. President Obama's stimulus plan directs $1.4 billion for re-training people to help find new jobs. But how can the 50+ ageing workers withstand this stress of losing jobs, and finding new ones with new skills?

Kelly White, 55, spent 30 years in the printing industry before losing her job. Then she registered in a Community college to be trained as an electronic service worker, for two years. In the end, she found she had no prospects of getting any job at all. At last, she found a job as a Schoolbus Driver with $13 per hour as wages.

Can the President Help?

Whether the HELP programme can help such job losers is a big question. All these four programmes are highly cost-intensive that need huge investments, and this is where the political skill of President Obama is tested. There are 45 million Americans who have no health insurance, and with job losses the situation will be worse. For the US Government, health insurance itself would cost $ One Trillion plus in the next ten years! There are many players involved in providing good health to Americans. First and foremost are the Doctors who want more money from the patients. Second, drug makers and medical device suppliers who also want to make money by aggressively selling their drugs and medical wares. The Hospitals are. not far behind in taking money from patients by imposing unwanted tests in collusion with Doctors and Specialists. According to the *New York Times*, 30 per cent of all healthcare spending in the USA — some $100 billion a year - is wasted on tests and treatment that do not improve the health of the patients. The poor patient comes last and s/he has nowhere to go for redressal, except to the grave!

Take the case of prostate cancer, which a large majority of the ageing population is likely to get. According to David Leonhardt, "No serious study has found that the high technology treatment do better at keeping men/women healthy and alive. Most die of something else before prostate cancer becomes a problem. Some doctors, with good intention of course, suggest what is called 'Watchful Waiting', which will cost a few thousand dollars more in follow up visits and tests.

Surgery to remove the prostate gland would cost about US$ 23,000. A targeted form of radiation, known as IMRT runs to $50,000. Proton radiation therapy often exceeds $100,000" (New York Times, July 2009) Then the Medical Insurance fellows will make the patients run around in vain!

Education, Labour and Pension have still more complicated problems. Teachers in basic schools are supposed to get their pay on performance of the learners, which is difficult.

In the early days, doctors and teachers were said to be away from the money temptation. For some it is still true, but not for the majority! The best of brains in the White House are struggling to make HELP succeed, but time alone will tell how much HELP is given to the Americans.

2

Yoga, Meditative and the Spiritual Living

Yoga Centers or Beauty Parlours ?

In 1998 when I was the UNICEF Representative in Bhopal, I had severe Spondylitis (neck and head pain) and by late evening it became unbearable. Yoga Ratna late Dr. Ganguli, a civil engineer by profession and a leading building contractor in those days in Bhopal, was regularly holding free Yoga classes for the young and old, men and women, girls and boys, from 6 to 8 am in a Town Hall spared by the Bhopal Municipal Corporation, free of charge. Dr. Ganguly was almost 70 years at the time and when I told him about my neck pain he asked for how long I was having it. I said, "four months" "Then you must come for four weeks at least to learn basic Yoga postures and *Pranayam.*" I agreed and we (my wife and I) attended his Yoga classes without fail for three months. Dr. Ganguli never charged a single rupee since he wanted to return to society what he got from it. He always said Patanjali's *Yoga Shastra* was for the wellbeing of humanity and not for making money. We have continued our yoga practice since then. *Shavasana* and *Shirshasana* are my favourite asanas among the lot, and I continue my yoga even today in this 73rd year of my birth!

Tragedy of a Market Approach

Yoga has spread around the world. In the US alone, as many as 16 millions are either teaching or practising yoga, and quite a few are making money out of it. There are as many as 1000 yoga centres of all types - some for selling health and beauty care, some for treating ailments, and some really for spiritual rejuvenation. "Om" has been turned into a money spinner! However, Sybil Killian, General Manager for the OM Yoga Centre in Manhattan, New York, questioned whether yoga could fairly claim to be a spiritual pursuit when, according to an industry estimate, it earns US$ 6 billion a year in the US alone! *(New York Times Report).*

Ten years ago, with yoga transforming into a pop culture phenomena, teachers across the US joined together to create a voluntary online registry of yoga training schools to meet new standards. One cannot develop any standards for Yoga. If we go through Patanjali's *Yoga Shastra,* there are as many as 6000 postures and methods and over the ages, Yoga Gurus in India at least taught them as a matter of spiritual wellbeing and harmonising the mind and body at the same me. Yogasanas are not gym exercises performed by listening to pop music and TV. That is the whole tragedy in the US. Yoga has been taught as a body exercise than as an instrument of body-mind harmonisation. *Om shanty, shanty, shanty...* will not lead your mind to tranquility if you are just doing Yoga as an exercise.

Because the yoga teachers went online, the regulators in the US thought it a big business that has to be regulated and taxed.

The regulators say by licensing these Yoga Centres, the yoga class entrepreneurs would observe basic standards and protect customers who usually spend US$ 2000 to $ 4000 on getting to know the postures and methods like *Pranayarna.* "If you are starting a Yoga school and taking money from the customers, you should play by a set of rules," says a Wisconsin licensing official.

Because of this fear of licensing, the yoga entrepreneurs are uniting against the State - their common enemy. But once yoga turns into a market-friendly enterprise, we cannot capture the spirit of *Yoga Shastra.* A day will come when certain postures will be patented by a certain yoga teacher in the US and then those postures will be sold under a patented copyright DVDs! How can you patent Patanjali's thousands of postures and make them an Intellectual property of a particular yoga teacher? This is the absurdity of market-based growth to spiritual development! God save Patanjali!

Relevance of Sant Basaveshwara in the 21st Century

No religion preaches violence. Unfortunately, terrorism is on the rise in the name of religion. Hence the need of the day is to tell the world the real meaning of religion — to spread the message of peace, tolerance, kindness and universal brotherhood. And this is what Sri Taralabalu Jagadguru Brihanmath strives for...

Karnataka is known for many Lingayat Maths, which have over the years promoted numerous educational, cultural and religious activities. However, a few Swamijis who head these Maths have made their own fortunes, often forgetting the teachings of the 12th century Saint Jagatjyoti Basaveshwara, which they proclaim to spread. The recently concluded 9 - day long Taralabalu Hunnime Festival (Feb. 10-18) organised by the Taralabalu Brihanmath of Sirigere in Karnataka, in the sprawling

Palace grounds of Bengaluru where lakhs of people gathered, was a missed opportunity for spreading the teachings of Basaveshwara in this 21st century of terrorism, greedy capitalism, global warming, biological warfare, and what have you! According to some surveys by think-tanks like the World Economic Forum, the biggest threat of this century is fear and insecurity, not poverty. India is shining, but it is also showing signs of decay, communal violence, death and disability in many tribal areas, and scams of the highest order. Temple-building mania is getting strong and we are witnessing the worst remnants of religious fundamentalism and bigotry.

Seek God Within, not Without

Against this background, we have to position the teachings of Basaveshwara and find answers to many of the 21st century ailments-not just national, but global as well. Basavanna was a reformer par excellence and his was the religion of humanity (not linked to any caste or creed) and his entire philosophy was centred on reforming the 'Human Beings' in their entirety - from their economic wellbeing to spiritual enlightenment to their central role in governing the affairs of the society. He stressed the importance of the three Hs - Head (knowledge/arivu), Heart (devotion) and the Hands (work/*'kayaka).* 'Work is worship' (*kayaka ve kailash)* was his road to Divinity and prosperity. Poverty cannot be removed by slogans - as our present day politicians do - but through work and wellbeing. There is no need for temple worship.

The Vishwa Hindu Parishad diehards should learn from Basavanna, who was born in a Brahmin family, that to see Ram we need not build a Ram temple in Ayodhya. In one of his famous.

Sri Taralabalu Jagadguru Brihanmath is a well known religious centre in Karnataka. Taralabalu' means 'long live, my son'.

These are the words used by Vishwabandhu Marulasiddha, the founder of this Peetha, while blessing his follower Telagubalu Siddaiah to occupy the pontifical seat. Marulasiddha fought against ignorance, blind belief and the barren traditions prevalent in the 12th century. 'Long live, my Son' is not meant to a single individual but to the whole of mankind.

This Peetha is eight-century old and Marulasiddha was an enlightened contemporary of Basaveshwara. In order to commemorate this day, Taralabalu Hunnime Mahotsava is celebrated in different parts of the country annually on the full moon day of the month of Magha. This celebration is on the lines of national integration, universal brotherhood and strives to teach mankind that all religions are one and have the common purpose of making man to cultivate the values of life in every walk of everyday life.

Vachanas (sayings), Basavanna talks about the culture of building temples and going there to seek God's blessings:

"The rich build temples, Shiva,
What shall I, poor man, do, my Lord?
My legs are the pillars,
My body the shrine,
And my head, the Golden Pinnacle!
Oh, Lord Kudala Sangama,
Things standing shall fall
But the moving ever shall stay."

Rama is within us and not in the temples, and so is Shiva in our heart and soul to worship and meditate at alltimes.

Worth of Women

Basavanna was the first to recognise the value of women in our society and in all his *Vachanas* he has elevated the status of women and condemned the Brahmanical treatment of women by denying their right to worship in temples, right to participate in all religious programmes, rebuilding the family and the society. His time also witnessed the emergence of women saints like Akka Mahadevi, who embodied the virtues of ideal womanhood. In the 21st century, women participating in politics will be crucial, and they would assert their rights - in governance, business and in all walks of life.

The organisers of the Taralabalu Hunnime Festival in Bengaluru, despite being guided by the present Head of the Brihanmath, Dr. Shivamurthy Swamiji an internationally known scholar on religion and philosophy lost the opportunity to spread the great healing message of Basava during these nine days. The passion of talking on Basavanna and what he did for the poor and the downtrodden, as was being done for almost four decades by the late His Holiness Shivakumar Swamiji of Brihanmath, was missing. I instead the organisers honoured the corrupt politicians of the State with all fanfare, and thus brought a bad name to this great festival for human harmony. Bengaluru is an international city and eminent scientists and technologists could have been invited to share their ideas on how to empower the poor through science and technology, and not through the rhetoric of fraudulent politics.

A 21st Century Saint with a Difference

Our country is known for hundreds of dharma gurus, spiritual icons, meditational saints and what have you! The diversity of religion, caste and creed, even after hundreds of years, has continued today, despite the equalising technologies and globalisation, supposed to bring about change in our social structure and values. The message of social equality and a casteless society propounded by the 12th century Saint Basaweshwara of South India, like Saint Kabir in North India, is still relevant in this 21st century.

In Karnataka there are many Veerashiva Mutts which claim to spread the message of Saint Basava, but the most iconic is Dr. Sree Sree Shivakumara Swamiji of Siddaganga Mutt in Tumkur, whose 105th birthday, themed 'Work as Worship', was observed as a Guruvandana programme on April 28, 2012, where hundreds of his devotees, admirers, politicians, and the poverty-struck deprived peasants, were present to pay their respects. Smt. Sonia Gandhi flew from New Delhi to offer her Guruvandana to this Saint of Karnataka.

Politicians in Karnataka have been vying for his blessings over the years, and just as the wicked and the holy, good and bad, thieves and the honest, flock to a temple for God's blessings, so is the case with Swamiji, who keeps blessing one and all. But the politicians in Karnataka have exploited his blessings, not for doing good to the poor and the needy, but for their greed and glamour. The BJP leaders in Karnataka were dubbed as the greatest beneficiaries of the blessings of Swamiji. The Congress leaders felt left behind and this time they blocked out all others and took a lead to get blessings for the All India Congress Party. Smt Sonia Gandhi offered her *pranams* with a garland to Swamiji and the Celebration Committee managed to offer her, as the blessings of Swamiji, a saree worth Rs. 50, 000 - a gesture the poor women of Karnataka felt jealous of! The Karnataka Congress leaders also presented Swamiji a purse of Rs. 105 lakh to coincide with his 105th birth year.

Service Sans Segregation

As he gets into the 105th year of his service to mankind, Swamiji hardly sleeps for a few hours, does not wear spectacles to read books, does *puja* for hours, and supervises the wellbeing of thousands of kids studying in more than 120 educational institutes from Kindergarten to PhD. In the last 70 years of his untiring service, he believed in promoting Universal Human

Values through Four Bs among the youth of the country - viz, *budhi* (knowledge), *baduku* (work as worship), *bhava* (emotional strength), and *bhakti* (devotion to the Almighty) — cutting across caste and creed. Children from all religions and classes have studied in schools of the Mutt and imbibed secular values. As many as 7000 boys are fed daily, apart from thousands of devotees who visit to seek his blessings. Swamiji personally supervises the kitchen. The Siddaganga Institute of Technology (SIT) is completing 50 years of educational excellence in 2013.

In his benediction to MBA students of SIT Swamiji once said, "The social reformer of 12th century, Lord Basaweshwara said: 'With the strength of knowledge, ignorance fades away; with the strength of light, darkness fades away; with the strength of truth, lie fades away.'" These inspiring words always keep the students here from ragging and violent activities on the campus. On the Graduation Ceremony of the Students of SIT, Swamiji made them repeat these words of wisdom from the *Thaittiriya Upanishad:* "Speak the truth; Live righteously; Don't stop self-learning and scholarly discourse; Don't cut the human chain of God's Creation. If you have something to give, give that with faith, grace, humility, and with understanding. This is the Command. This is the Instruction."

Swamiji is a moving spirit for the staff, students and their parents from all over India and abroad, who feel proud to send their kids here to study. He was worried over the cost of firewood in the Mutt's kitchen and was feeling anxious about the depleting firewood from the forest. Now the kitchen has moved to solar energy, installed with 110 Scheffler dishes, contributing to the saving of about Rs. 15.75 lakh from its current fuel bill of Rs. 22.5 lakhs with 300 days of operation per annum.

Dr. Sree Sree Shivakumara Swamiji is the present head of Sree Siddaganga Mutt in Tumkur District, South India, and founder of the Sree Siddaganga Education Society. He was born in Veerapura near Magadi Taluk. He is proficient in English, Kannada and Sanskrit. He has established educational institutions which offer courses in the traditional learning of Sanskrit as well as in modern science and technology. Swamiji's 'Guru Kula' houses more than 8500 children of age group 5 to 16 years and is open to children from all religions, castes, and creeds, who are provided free food, education, and shelter. Under the pontiffs guidance, an annual agricultural fair is held for the benefit of the local population. He is widely respected for his philanthropic work by all communities. In recognition of his humanitarian work, Swamiji was conferred an honorary degree of Doctor of Literature by the Karnataka University in 1965. Swamiji was awarded the Prestigious Karnataka Ratna award, the highest civilian award given by Karnataka Government, on his centenary year 2007, for his social service. He continues his humanitarian work even at the age of 105.

Osho International Meditation

"One has to become old, and when you are becoming old reluctantly, old age becomes ugly. When you become old Joyously, old age has a beauty of its own, a grandeur, ripeness, maturity, and a centering."
Osho on 'ageing'

It was an early morning in a summer day when my wife and I reached the Osho Meditation Centre in Koregaon Park, Pune, with prior reservation. After the routine security checks, the escort took us to the fascinating Osho Guesthouse where telephones, liquids, solids and eatables are banned! Everything is disciplined here. At 9 am, as newly arrived guests, we had to undergo an HIV test! The Osho Resort was the first in India to impose the HIV tests, almost two decades back, to all the inmates who wish to stay in the resort. Why? Osho had reasoned, "HIV/ AIDS is the disease of the civilisation, and given the freedom of all to live as they pleased in the resort, including free sex, it was made compulsory for all visitors, young and old, to make sure they did not suffer from this deadly disease!" Couples like us, in the twilight of our lives, may revolt or at best laugh away such tests at our age! But we had to undergo it, anyway!

Having got our ID cards, we were asked to put on the mandatory pink robes, and not our kurta pyjama or sari. Here the business starts-these robes cost a steep Rs. 500, and once you are out of the resort, they are useless! Luckily, in our case, the guesthouse manager gave them on rent, and we escaped the expenses!

Know Yourself

Then the orientation starts for all the new inmates. The first session was induction in the dynamic meditation of Osho: "Meditation means bliss in being alone. One is really alive when one has become capable of it, when there is no dependence anymore on anybody, on any situation, on any condition. It is something welling up within you!" The young volunteers (in our case, an engineering graduate) taught us dynamic meditation through computer simulated music and visuals. Osho preached many types of meditation, such as Kundalini, Whirling, Vipasana, and Gowrishankar. He also clarified, "there are no such things as meditational techniques. In the end, techniques vanish and you gradually understand what you are. And if you become aware, then you have known yourself." (Osho's book, *Meditation: The First and the Last Freedom)* In the present computer generated music and dance, an elderly couple like us cannot dance, but just watching the young mad crowd was itself a relaxation! Osho was a pragmatist and said meditation is not concentration or attention which creates tension! The very sound of the word 'concentration' gives us a feeling of tenseness!

The resort has the best of ambience, with solitary green and shady sit-outs and relaxation and meditating corners, as well as spas and swimming pools-catering to the needs of all age groups. The restaurants are managed by trained nutritionists and one has to buy coupons (no cash is accepted) by paying cash while registering as a guest in the beginning. The best part was listening to Osho in the big Vipasana Hall where you have to wear white robes. Again, you have to buy them, and a cash-starved visitor will go mad in wearing these mandatory pink and white robes in and out. I don't think Osho, who believed in the freedom of an individual, imposed these 'robes discipline'. The worldwide disciples and managers who run this Ashram must rethink about this and allow the freedom to wear simple clothes.

When we sat in the big Vipasana Hall, Osho's video-recorded talk was played, and for an hour or so, all the inmates of the Resort were spellbound. In his lifetime, Osho had read almost 100,000 books of all religions and faiths, and as a result, his talks were mesmerising and thought-provoking, full of anecdotes and humour - always highlighting the realism in life. I have read hundreds of his books and heard many of his CDs. Sue Appleton, Attorney in the Supreme Court of Victoria, says "Bhagwan Shree Rajneesh (famously called 'Osho') was the most dangerous man since Jesus Christ!" He was dubbed a 'sex guru' because Osho was merciless about society's double standards on sex. And his assertion, that sexual repression resulted in sexual obsession, outraged the conservative Indians and religious heads! In fact, many in those days believed that Osho guided his followers to redirect their sexual energy towards spiritual fulfillment.

As we checked out from the Osho Resort after 30 hours of stay, I remembered Osho telling about the Sufi Saint Farid, who did not accept a pair of golden and emerald scissors from King Akbar who wanted to honour him. Farid asked the King for a simple needle because he said scissor cuts, but the needle joins. He didn't want to cut, but join the hearts and minds of people!

Jai ho, Osho!

3

Travel and the Wilderness

Staying Young - A Science or an Art? Musings from a Cruise Ship to Alaska

My wife and I were on the cruise ship 'Coral Princess' as it sailed into the Alaskan Sea in the sunny summer month of May 2004. The ship's 2000 passengers comprised largely of elderly American couples with very few nationals of other countries. Perhaps at 67 and 58, we were the youngest couple on board. The cruise ship had great chefs who produced 10,000 meals a day and served gallons of wine and drinks to the old and the occasional young.

The ship's Buddha lounge and swimming pool had some elderly Japanese who were doing their meditation to Om music against the background of the serene Alaskan sea. I started my yoga in a corner and after some postures and pranayamam, did Shirsasana. After I had finished, I went into the Jacuzzi. An 80-year-old American entered the Jacuzzi and asked me about yoga and how I could stand on my head without support and bend my body in the postures.

The conversation veered towards ageing issues, the lifestyle diseases of the Americans and how Americans are trying to stay young. Stating that the mind is the cause of ailments, I pointed out that yoga and meditation do not cost anything but mechanised gyms are capital intensive. Now the question was: How do Americans learn the twin techniques of yoga and meditation? Today, there are a large number of ageing adults in America and their favourite topic, whether on the beach or on a cruise is how to stay young.

"Every man desires to live long but no man would be old," wrote Jonathan Swift. Faced with the ever-present ticking clock, can a healthy middle-aged man tell if he is likely to remain free of the disabling diseases which often tarnish the golden years? To find out, American scientists evaluated 6,505 men between the ages of 45 and 68 who were in good health when the study began in the mid-'60s as part of the famed Honolulu heart programme. Of the men who survived to reach ages between 71 and 95, 40 per cent remained free of both physical and cognitive impairment. The best predicators of successful ageing were low blood pressure, low blood sugar, abstinence from tobacco.

A Walk around the Robben Island

I was lucky to visit the Robben Island where Nelson Mandela was jailed for 22 years, on my recent trip to Cape Town in South Africa. It is now a historical place visited by thousands of tourists.

As my wife and I took the boat to the Robben Island in Cape Town, my thoughts went back to Nelson Mandela's classic, *Long Walk to Freedom* (1994), which he wrote soon after he was sworn in as President of the Republic of South Africa. On his long stay in the prison, he says, "A prison is designed to break one's spirit and destroy one's resolve. Prison authorities exploit every weakness, demolish every initiative, negate all signs of individuality-all with the idea of stamping out that spark that makes each of us human and each of us who we are. The authorities kept us flocked, but it helped reinforce our determination. We regarded the struggle in prison as a microcosm of the struggle as a whole. We would fight inside as we would fight outside. We had no toilets and we just had iron buckets known as 'bailies' and it had a lid with some water stored for washing hands and faces. The bailies had to be cleaned in the sinks at the end of the corridor to avoid stench. This was one moment when we could whisper to each other because the Warden never came there due to the dirty smell! Robben Island was known as a University because of what we learned from each other, and we made a distinction between academic studies which were official, and political studies which were not ...!"

In his recent book, *Conversation with Myself* (2010), Mandela says to his Jailor, "I made an application 10 months ago in September 1968, for leave to attend my mother's funeral. Approval of that application would have been a generous act on your part and would have made a deep impression on me. On July 13, 1969, my eldest son Madiba, 24, died in an accident. You didn't allow me to see his face ..."

Both these volumes are classic pieces of human suffering and show how a great leader can withstand the torture because of the leadership passion he possesses.

Robben Island, which means 'Seal Island', was declared a World Heritage Site on December 1997, and now functions as a museum and serves as a reminder and tribute to the courage of people who fought against a racist regime at their own peril.

Freedom Island

When we got down from the boat to reach the famous prison cells of hundreds of political prisoners, we were delighted to enter the bus driven by 'Freedom'! *Suddenly, I wanted to name this place 'Freedom Island'!* We were shocked when the tour guide announced how the prisoners were used as slaves to work in the limestone quarry to extract lime and other toxic materials without regard to their eyesight and health. Many prisoners suffered due to these long hours of work in the quarries.

We also saw a beautiful Church where two types of flags were hoisted when there was a birth — reported by mothers who were separated from husbands in the cells. A green flag for a boy, and red for girl! At least those prisoners, separated from their pregnant wives, would feel great when they saw these flags... What a human cruelty!

When we saw the cell where prisoner No. 466/64 (even now Mandela calls himself by that number) was confined, we were further horrified. The apartheid regime ensured that all political prisoners were not even allowed to see Nature-the roaring ocean, the waves and its delightful sands on the Robben Island, by building huge walls around their cells. When we were shown a piece of land where Mandela used to grow vegetables for his fellow prisoners, the guide, himself a political prisoner here earlier, was almost in tears.

When the food in the prison was neither nutritious nor tasty, Mandela asked the jail authorities to provide a piece of land to grow vegetables; he was snubbed and the request was rejected. Memos were sent up and down, lawyers were consulted. After six months, he was allowed a piece of land. Mandela started digging and found bones, which he broke into powder to use as fertiliser. But he was suspected and was stopped. They presumed by digging up bones Mandela was trying to show prisoners had been secretly buried on Robben Island! Later, the jail authorities relented and gave him proper fertilisers for his garden.

On our way back to the boat for Cape Town, we got into conversation with an elderly Afrikaner, and I asked him whether he had ever met Mandela. He said he used to be a political prisoner, was fond of Mandela and had shaken his hand. On what he thought about Mandela. he said: "Life, love and courage are his legacy for the Afrikaner." He greeted me with an Afrikaans phrase, *gesondheid* (Cheers)! I reciprocated, "Long live Nelson Mandela!"

Travails of Travel in Devabhoomi

This 'Abode of Gods' in no mathc for 'God's own Country' in being tourist-friendly.

The Himalayan State of Uttarkhand, also known as Uttaranchal. is an exotic land of mountain creeks, valleys and clouds kissing the peaks, to enchant the holidayers, itinerant tourists or semi-naked Sadhus wandering across the mountain roads and creeks with awe and joy... But the joy of riding a bus of taxi may be short-lived if we are stuck in a long queue of buses waiting for the landslide to be cleared by the Border Roads Organisation. The roads are the nerve centre of Uttarkhand, and it is amazing how the truckers, bus drivers, motorists, and taxt drivers keep on smiling and wishing eacn other good luck while driving, unlike the city drivers in Mumbai and Bengaluru where load rage is the norm.

Our taxi drive from Haridwar to Joshimath took almost 12 hours and then we were to drive up to the Cliff Top Club Resort in Auli, 12000 ft above the sea level, from where you can see the Nandi Devi of the Himayaias We had booked accommodation for a week. This is an RCI resort and the Club in its published booklet had stated it will provide pickup from Joshimath or that we take the Ropeway which closes at 4 pm. The telephones don't work at this height and we have to Keep on praying to get connected Our taxi driver was reluctant to drive on this stretch of 10 km because of big creeks. But somehow we reached the Club after our Tata Indica taxi got damaged a little on the way.

The Manager of the Club, as usual was amongetic and when I informed him that the M.P of Joshimath has a Rs. 2 crores budget under the MP's Local Area Development Scheme (MPLAD) for improving such roads, someone pointed out. The politics involved in doing this, if the road is developed, the Ropeway will have fewer passengers to commute, resulting in losses for this public sector undertaking! The Ropeway charges Rs. 500 for each trip — to come up from Joshimath and return from the Cliff Top. The lift provided in the Cliff Top stop on the Ropeway is non-functional, and the elderly have to climb 150 iron steps, and any slip means you end up with broken ribs and legs!

The Gharwal Mandal Vikas Nigam (GMVN) has to promote tourism with lots of professionalism, just as Kerala has promoted itself as 'God's Own Country'. In fact, the presence of God is felt all the time by the tourists in Devabhoomi because one gets scared by the deep curves the bus and taxi drivers have to negotiate.

The best part of the trekking is the way the horsemen help us enjoy the ride on a horseback. Here again, the tourists are never told in advance that you have to pay an entrance fee if you trek in the protected reserve forest. When I returned from the horse trekking, the forest guard came to collect Rs. 40 as entrance fee!

Information is the essence of good tourism, crucial to both young and old. Tourists must know every detail of the beauty of the spots and Good smiling faces of the Gharwalis are no substitute for informed tourism. God save Devabhoomi.

Pleasures and Pains of Global Travel

Planning is not enough, assurances form your travel agent may not be good enough and you can be meticulous about your journey and yet land in a mess. This is the first of a two part travelogue.

My wife and I keep travelling, first during my job in UNICEF (the United Nations Children's Fund), and then after retirement. For almost a decade now, we have been travelling to places of interest - some of them worth writing about, some just for memorable pictures for grand children, spots of scenic beauty or simply on food and wine journeys.

We had planned this present trip to Norweigh and then to USA almost six months in advance. On the eve of our departure, my travel agent in Bangalore called to tell us that the Air India flight from Mumbai was delayed by 12 hours, which, in turn, would affect our onward connecting flight to Oslo by British Air. So here it was - a journey well planned was taking off with the prospect of loosing our hotel reservation in Oslo and a British Air connection that was not refundable if we missed the flight. My travel agent quickly decided to put us on board Sri Lanka airlines to London so that we could catch our flight to Oslo. Lesson Number One: No point in planning too much in advance, particularly if you are travelling by Air India with a frequent flyer temptation, where your flying credits are anyhow never credited in time. Air India has grim looking air hostesses who never smile, nor do they serve you well! Our first time experience of travelling by Sri Lanka airlines was great because we were put in a beach hotel in Colombo at no extra cost!

We boarded the Sri Lanka airlines flight to London at Colombo and enjoyed the great hospitality of the airlines. We had seen the statutes of laughing Buddha in Colombo but witnessing the service by smiling air hostesses was just great and stood out in contrast to Air India! After about 12 long hours, we landed at London. We had to pick up our luggage at London's Heathrow airport to check in for our connecting British Airways flight to Oslo. But all checked-in bags are picked up *after the immigration counter.* We had no transit visa at London even to get through the immigration just to pick our luggage; our travel agent had advised us that there was no need for a transit visa if we had a multiple entry US Visa. But the immigration counter at London's Heathrow is a nightmare and the immigration *babus* said we ought to have a transit visa. They took away our passports and all the tickets, and asked us to sit as prisoners till they "enquire" - we waited with bated breath, tense and uneasy. I showed my UN photo identity as a retiree, they browsed our visas to the United States and Norwiegh. We sat almost for two hours with no water and no access to a toilet! Then I was allowed to use a nearby phone. I thought of calling my brother in London but I had no coins. I took out my Master Card and got through but in a fit of nervousness/excitement, I forgot my HSBC Master Card. By the time I realised this, it was too late. To our agony was now added another worry. Then, at last, our passports were stamped for exit and we were allowed to leave the immigration section to pick up our luggage. Lesson Number Two: To avoid the transit visa at Heathrow Airport, either avoid checking your bags and have only hand bags or book your luggage to your final destination right at the beginning of your journey. Travel agents will never know the immigration rules, which keep changing, and UK transit visa fees are exorbitant.

Just when we picked up our luggage and went to check in at the British Airways counter to catch our Oslo flight, we were harassed by an Indian check-in assistant for excess baggage payment. We agreed to pay 30 pounds through an American

Express card, which would not accept the charge! Then, we virtually collected all our quarter cents from our pockets and paid the excess baggage charges and collected our boarding passes and rushed to board the Oslo Flight. Lesson Number Three: Avoid taking too much luggage and travel light so that you can check in and out very fast without increasing your blood pressure! Because of the threat of terrorism, security procedures can be rather tight.

Seniors are not free from these excruciating security checks. The British Airways flight to Oslo is about an hour and odd, and my wife was pleased to get her vegetarian snacks on board. Vegetarians have a problem in global travel although all airlines do provide veggie meals if only you tell them in advance. We reached Oslo late evening. Next stop: Hotel, but a hurdle remained. We went to get Norwegian currency (NOKs) but the bank was closed! We asked about the cheapest way to reach our hotel — taxi was the costliest and bus was the cheapest and the best. But how will you pay when you have no NOKs? The bus driver said we could pay by credit card but my Amex Card did not click at London! I took out a Stan Chart debit card which, to our surprise, worked. We chanted 'Jai Mata' as we got onto the bus and within thirty minutes were in best western hotel in Oslo- a nice, warm, Norwegian welcome was waiting for us. Lesson Number Four: Please carry as many credit cards as you can. If one does not work, use another and move on.

We booked the "Norweigh in a Nutshell" tour the next morning and the train from Oslo to Bergen (450 kms) was fascinating in the sense that the tour combines rail, ship (to see the famous Fjords of Norweigh) and bus (to see the valleys and then back to Oslo or Bergen). There are about 140 railway lines in Western Europe and these have been evaluated in terms of adventure. Only 19 of the mountain lines are awarded three stars, which is the top mark. Two of these three star lines are to be found in Norway - the Bergen Railway and Flam Railway, which are the most impressive mountain lines in the world. Nearly 80 per cent of the 20 km long Flam railway has a gradient of 55 per cent and the smallest curve radius is only 130 meters. Railway experts are thrilled abut this railway line!

The Flam railway crosses the Flam valley and the flam river three times without the use of a single bridge. Instead of building bridges, the engineers have led the river in the tunnels through the mountains under the railway tracks. This is the wonder of the Norwegian Flam railway.

Senior citizens are respected everywhere in Norweigh in terms of rail and bus tariff and overall respect perhaps because it is a country of seniors! In Oslo, we saw the famous park where granite statues of a crying child, a happy couple, and a happy family are installed which depict the peaceful Norwegian society. The Town Hall in Oslo, where the Noble Peace Prize is awarded is an architectural beauty. In Bergen, we saw the magnificent view of the sprawling harbour from the ropeway. Our four day Oslo-Bergen trip ended when we took the flight to London-New York by Virgin Airlines. This time, we booked our luggage straight to New York to avoid the harassment at Heathrow harassment over a transit visa! Lesson Number Five: Check from your airlines, if you are combining more than one airline, whether you can book your luggage to the final destination right in the beginning. Do a lot of research on baggage checking rules of different airlines; don't leave this to travel agents.

Reaching Newark Liberty International Airport (New Jersey) in USA where we joined our grandchildren was a big relief.

These snapshots of Seals during a boat trip make us worry about the dwindling species of our seaworld.

Dwindling Seals of Cape Town

As my wife and I took off to the Atlantic Ocean shores of Hout Bay in Cape Town on a sunny day in October 2010 to enjoy the beauty of the vanishing Seals, we were struck by their shining glitter and the beauty of the ocean.

Seals are found all over the world and there are 33 known species, falling into the category of animals known as 'pinnipeds'. The largest Seal can be 16 ft long and the smallest 4 ft. The males are called 'bulls' and the females 'cows', and the offsprings are termed 'pups'. They are very intelligent sea animals and have been known to bite and attack humans who get too close to them. They look like gentle creatures with brownish bodies and small heads, and as mammals they offer milk to the young pups until they are old enough to feed on their own. They are warm-blooded because of their layers of fat that keep them warm when necessary. They enjoy the humans who speed the ocean in boats.

The most common is the Grey Seal. There are Elephant Seals, Fur Seals, Sleeping Weddell Seal, Leopard Seal and Baby Harp Seal, but our tour guide could not identify the type we were seeing. But my curiosity made me ask a conservationist who was clicking the Seals with a highly sophisticated camera. He simply said, "Call them Hout Bay Seals"! He also said that in 1988 a type of distemper virus spread among the Seals, and resulted in the death of one-third of the group.

In spite of a big crowd in the boat and clicking of photos, we didn't find any movement in the sleeping and resting Seals. What do they eat? Mostly, they eat shellfish, salmon, mackerel, and shrimp. Seals are hunted by predators such as sharks and killer whales. Humans like us hunt for their oil, pelt and meat. A study has revealed that Seals of all types diet on 67 species of fish and 70 species of invertebrates.

Fishing the Oceans Dry

Worldwide, Seals are in danger of being extinct because of the dwindling oceanic food. There are 'seafood prints' like 'carbon footprints, which means dwindling of oceanic products like fish. Every year, more than 170 billion pounds of wild fish and shell fish are caught in our nets and fisheries managers all over the world call this a mass-hunted ocean catch. (See National Geographic, October 2010) It is not just humans eating fish. Tuna eat enormous amounts of fish and it is estimated that a large Tuna must eat the equivalent of its body weight every ten days to stay alive! A single thousand pound Tuna might need to eat as many as 15,000 smaller fish in a year! In addition to large fish eating the small fish, the worst is the excess catch by humans and big seafood corporates. According to the FAO, oceans don't have enough fish left to support the current onslaught.

In this whole oceanic fight for fish, how will our poor Seals find their food? What will they eat? How will they survive? Who will feed them? With these nagging questions, we bid goodbye to our Seals and returned to Hout Bay boat parking spot, feeling sorry for the Seals. God save them!

Beware of dog owners!

Those who walk their dogs without a leash are a menace to society but never admit it.

In residential colonies in many cities of India one invariably finds a board on the gate that says "Beware of Dog" even when there are no dogs! Thus the board itself has been deployed as a watchdog to scare away strangers and hawkers. I have seen such boards in my colony in Bengaluru even when there are no dogs in residence.

Dog owners who actually keep dogs often walk their pets without a leash. They tend to sniff at strangers, scaring them. If the owners is told to leash pets, the reply is invariably, "Don't worry, it won't bite. My John is very sweet!" Such dog owners are mannerless and careless.

Once I was walking with my six-year-old grandson and an unleashed dog jumped on me. I fell down, got hurt. My grandkid started crying. When I shouted at the owner's wife she shouted back, saying I had hit the dog, which is why it attacked me! My veterinary doctor says all dogs confined to houses are emotionally angry and jump on strangers at the slightest provocation.

Recently, our Pomeranian Jimmy died. In the 20 years he was with us, he was never allowed to go out without a leash. In the west you never see unleashed pets-all those without a leash are by definition street dogs and are supposed to be taken away. Bengaluru Bruhat Mahanagar Palike (BBMP) is struggling with thousands of stray dogs and every day we hear of stray dogs biting kids, either killing or injuring them. Sixty dog bites were recently reported on a single day in Bangalore KC Hospital. Animal-lovers like Maneka Gandhi do not allow the killing of the stray dogs and then we have this problem of irresponsible behaviour of dog-owners who don't leash them for their daily walk, scaring the elderly and the very young.

The world recently observed World Rabies Day. The Prime Minister of Denmark said, "We do not want a society where you cannot go walking with your child or poodle without risking an attack by dogs." Denmark is known for fighter dogs like Pitbull Terriers, Mastiffs and Rotwellers and the incidence of attacks on other pets and people has gone up. Denmark now has a canine policy in place. India is one of the leading countries where stray dogs take a heavy toll on kids and others. According to WHO India has nearly 20,000 rabies-related deaths annually and accounts for 36 per cent of global deaths. Indian cities are leading in dog-related deaths and injuries. But our animal-lovers want to defend the rights of stray dogs. If they are so fond of them why don't they keep them in their homes?

Dog-lovers have a primary responsibility to keep their pets in safe custody and vaccinate them just as they vaccinate their newborn kids. The average cost of rabies immunisation after suspicious animal bite is $40 in Africa and $49 in Asia. This post-exposure treatment is a major financial burden for most of the poor households in India who earn around Rs. 100 a day per person and these are the ones who are usually bitten by street dogs.

Compulsory registration of dogs by city municipalities is one way of knowing the domestic dog population. Any dog not registered has to be treated as a stray dog and taken to a dog shelter or put to sleep. Our religious heads keep and manage *gao shalas* (cow shelters) - they can just as well add 'dog *shalas*' to their religious activities! Third, there should be a law to enforce compulsory vaccination of registered dogs by city municipalities. Their owners have to be fined if they fail to vaccinate their dogs. Fourth, street vendors selling meat snacks should be made to take away the bones and leftovers without throwing them to street dogs.

4

Leadership for Inspiration and Development

A Leadership Pipeline for Our Country

As you read these musings, our new Lok Sabha may have come into effect, and there would be nothing new about its newly elected members - same old representatives with criminal backgrounds and opportunistic proclivities. Somnath Chatterjee, before he laid down the office of the speakership of the last Lok Sabha, was angry and upset over the behaviour of our MPs in the Lok Sabha and said, 'You don't deserve a single paise out of public money for wasting Parliament's time". The performance of the MLAs across the country is no better, and we have seen many instances of them manhandling each other in many State Assemblies. Everyone bemoans the lack of leadership among our Political Executives to manage our democracy, and when on 26/11 Mumbai was hit with terrorism, the media and the intellectual community went on shouting "Enough is Enough" and cried aloud on the need for effective leaders. We are getting leaders by default, not by design.

Inclusion and Exclusion

From Gram Sabha to Vidhan Sabha to the Lok Sabha, we have elected leaders who are incapable of steering this country towards growth and poverty removal. That is why Mahatma Gandhi felt the need to build leadership first at Gram Sabha and then move up the ladder to Vidhan Sabha and on to Lok Sabha. MPs and MLAs, despite the 73rd and 74th Constitutional Amendments, have never liked smart men and women to emerge from these panchayats and urban bodies to move up to the Vidhan Sabha and Lok Sabha. We have today as many as 9,75,000 women panchayat leaders, and out of them 8,50,000 belong to scheduled castes and tribes. This is primarily due to the 33 per cent reservation of seats to women stipulated in the Constitution. Bihar has taken the bold step of increasing the number of seats for women in panchayats to 50 per cent, and many States are following suit. Unlike the reserved constituency of the Lok Sabha seat, which will remain reserved for at least 3-4 terms, the reservation of seats in the case of women in panchayats is just for a year. That means, a good woman panchayat leader, despite her good work in her constituency, cannot contest from the same constituency, because that constituency will be converted to a general category seat. This is another obstacle created by our MPs and MLAs so that the same good woman cannot contest from the same constituency at least for 2-3 times to serve the people of her constituency. Just before the Lok Sabha elections, Kalpana Sharma of *The Hindu* reported how a small-town educated woman, running a beauty parlour in Rhotak in Haryana, has been elected as a Municipal Councillor and is doing a great job helping people. We have hundreds of such women across the country, but they never see the portals of Vidhan Sabha or the Lok Sabha.

Compared to the criminal background of our MPs and MLAs, our Panchayat/Muncipal Council members are less prone to engage in malpractices because they work closer to their voters in a limited locality, where their dealings catch on like forest fire. In their latest book, *Inclusion and Exclusion in Local Governance: Field Studies from Rural India,* George Mathew and B.S. Baviskar of the Institute of Social Sciences, New Delhi, capture the leadership roles of many outstanding rural women panchayat members from all parts of India. There are stories of many *Panchayat Patis* (husbands) running the show on behalf of their wives for some time, but finally these *Panchayt Patnis* (wives) take over and push aside their husbands; stories where SC/ST women have moved from their mudfloor to occupy the plastic chairs in the Panchayt offices; stories where a brave woman who replaced the local Zamindar in Andhra in her Panchayat was killed because the Zamindar could not see this lady occupying his chair.

The corporate India talks of "talent pipeline" and "supply chain" and how they affect the performance of their enterprises. Similarly, there is need to talk about what this author calls leadership pipeline' to strengthen our democracy and good governance at all levels of this diverse country. Let smart young men and women from the Gram Sabhas and Nagar Sabhas of this complex country occupy the seats in Vidhan Sabhas, the Lok Sabha and the Rajya Sabha so that the leadership of this country is built from the grassroots.

Generation Gap is a Myth!

At this stage, the parents may be in 50s and the grandparents in 70s. The religious texts have divided the maximum lifespan of 100 years into 4 equal parts, namely *Brahmacharya, Grahastha, Vanaprastha,* and *Sanyas.* It was considered proper for persons past 50 to give up all activities of earning, and allow their grownup children to take, over the responsibilities. At this stage, the grandparents enjoy the company of their grandchildren, help them grow, and also do some social service. After 75, they shall leave family and society for Sanyas, and go to the jungle to meditate and do *tapssya* for salvation. This appears to be a scientific as well practical division of time and work for life. I find it quite relevant and meaningful even today.

Consumerism vs values: Unfortunately, the extreme materialism in the present day has made the modern society devoid of any serious values. The passion for consumerism has seen a burial of feelings of understanding, mutual respect and sacrifice for each other. A spirit of competition and exploitation is dominant everywhere.

Today, people worship wealth like God. They amass wealth, not only for their own lives, but to leave enough for the next 10 generations. They do not remember the wise old man's saying: "If son is capable, why earn more to leave for him, because he himself will earn a lot. And if the son is not capable, he will squander all that you leave, hence why leave?" This saying is full of wisdom, but not heeded by most. They continue to be involved in material and worldly pleasures. They insist on controlling their children and grandchildren. They are hardly allowed to enjoy their own freedom, use their own brains or follow their likings. The natural outcome of such domineering behaviour by grandparents will be an atmosphere of mutual differences, constant conflicts and friction in the house. In such a situation, if elders are physically weak, sick or handicapped, their problems become multifold. They naturally become victims of utter humiliation and complete neglect. The respect has already been lost by their own behaviour!

For Peaceful Co-existence

In a global scenario, specially in the West, I have met old

people with tears in their eyes-cursing themselves, or being neglected. The life's finale is being spent either in their homes with children, under a constant feeling of humiliation, or in old age homes, or they are forced to spend the fag end of their lives in hospitals where the children visit them casually, only to say "hello" with a bouquet of flowers. Such parents, and for that matter all parents, are forced to be selfish in their financial matters, or forced to earn even at this age. It is necessary to analyse this painful situation, the causes giving rise to it and to find solutions to tackle it. A dialogue between the elders and the youngsters will really be worthwhile and welcome.

Finally, I recommend a joint family system where possible, because it is the best for everyone's emotional, physical and financial support and security. Mutual respect, freedom of thought, action and financial independence are the pre-condition for a peaceful and comfortable old age in the company of the younger generation. However, if you do not agree with this, it may be better to have an independent arrangement, so as to maintain peace and freedom all around.

Generation X vs Generation Y

Today the world is witnessing a new boom of the young generation, Generation Y defined as those born between 1970 to 1990. And a new demographic situation is emerging where Generation X - the elderly born in the 30s to 50s - will have to struggle to face this Generation Y in several ways. Generation Y is also called 'Facebook generation' or Twitter generation' or Wikileaks generation', and Generation X is termed by some as 'Generation Zero' as well! As we move in this fast world, there is bound to be conflict of ideas, processes and behaviour between Generation X and Y.

Generation Y believes in tech-solutions and this is now revealed in what is called 'love at first byte' - an online dating behaviour of the young. Unlike Generation X who believed in what was called in those days as 'love at first sight', Generation Y believes in online dating because there is no time to meet face to face.

Blowing cyber kisses have become a popular pastime even among the young Indian techies. According to E-Harmony, a prominent online dating service outfit, in a survey conducted on its behalf by Harris Interactive - a market research firm in the US-as many as 542 people were getting married everyday in the US, between the start of 2008 and the end of June 2009. E-Harmony claims to have accounted for almost 4.8 per cent of all American marriages in that period.

In another survey of 3,000 young Americans with romantic partners, it was found the Internet had become the third most common way of making initial contact - behind introductions from friends, but almost on par with encounters in bars and restaurants. In India, *Shaadi.com* and *Bharat Matrimony* can boast of millions of young clients, and these have become big hits with the young Indians who want to influence the choice of their marriage partners. The critics of this digital dating say this is a business built on the back of broken hearts, ruined marriages and damaged families. In the wake of globalisation and fast track ambition, Generation Y has faced many marital problems. We have such family patterns emerging like the Living Apart Together (LAT) couples, Double Income and No Kids (DINK) couples, and Divorced and Single Again (DASA) Couples. Now sexting is more famous than texting among the Generation Y! Y is also virulent on corruption issues as was seen in the wake of Cairo and Libyan youth against despotic and corrupt rule, and Anna Hazare's fast unto death on tackling corruption in India.

Age Considers, Youth Ventures

The lives of Generation X differ in living, behaviour, and in companionship. Is there a way to share the experience of

Generation X with the Generation Y, not on romance but on how to search one's companion and live together and not live as LAT couples? The digital age has started treating 'men and women, boys and girls' as a digital camera, described by the megapixels and other technical features to tempt the customer to buy it. God has created humans in a complex manner and no one individual on earth resembles another. That is the beauty of the humans and the products of nature.

Generation X are facing many problems of health, loneliness, companionship and emotional support. SMS and digital technologies cannot give them the missing human touch.

Although digital technologies are embraced by Generation Y much faster than Generation X, Generation X are still working in many enterprises, and the retirement age is likely to be raised to 70 in the West, where there is shortage of Generation Y. A recent study by the Kauffman Foundation in the US found that the 55-64 age-bracket have launched more businesses than those aged 20-34 every year since 1996.

In order to get the best from the human resources in our society, we have to treat both Generation X and Y as complementary and not competitive. Age shall not whither the Generation X! Three things can be promoted by our Society, whether in the East or the West, North or South. First, treat Generation X as mentors. Second, Generation X may respond to different incentives, but at the end their interest is not money but recognition. Nobody retires as such and retirement has, to be treated as a 'process' than an event. Second careers and 'bridge jobs' are now catching up with Generation X. Many enterprises are treating Generation X as 'just-in-time' work force that can be used to cope with the surging demand for hands, or to fill in the absent colleagues. God bless both Generation X and Y!

Admire the Old and Inspire the Young

Since my retirement from UNICEF in 1998 as a Development Professional I was looking for a second career more to share my experience with the young and the emerging talent in the country and so I took up a teaching job. For the last three years I have been teaching the MBA Students specialising in Human Relationships and its Management. (HRM) it is worth sharing my experience because senior citizens are taking up second career jobs in many areas.

Thanks to Dignity Foundation for exploring second career jobs for the "old" who still feel "young" to work. Some like me feel like "giving back" to the society more to feel good and great than get compensated. In the US the second career is called "Encore Career". Marc Freedman in the US wrote the famous book *Encore: Finding work that Matters in the Second Half of Life.*

Freedman says that a new life stage emerges after one's main career is completed but before infirmity sets ! That may be for some people just after 40 years when they decide to quit their main jobs to take up challenging work benefiting the society and the marginalised people. They do not wait till 60 or 65 to retire. The famous case is that of Bill Gates, the founder of Microsoft, said good bye to Microsoft and founded the Bill and Melinda Gates Foundation to bring cures for the tropical diseases like Malaria, TB and the most dreaded disease of the civilisation called HIV/AIDS .

Giving back need not necessarily be in terms of cash and it can be in terms of "inspiration" "empowerment" and a "pat on the back". At present there is a perception problem among the old and the young. In a second career the old generally make many mistakes of glorifying their past careers and their work, mesmerising and mystifying their "achievements", how they faced poverty, how they fought with their bosses and so on. Past is dead and gone, the young wants to know how they can do better in life, how can they got good jobs, what skills help them, and what are the time tested societal values which they can imbibe from the old. Very often I have seen many oldies sermonize the young and the young are easily bored and they keep avoiding the old. This is much more so among the retired bureaucrats and if we talk with them the first thing we hear is about is their fight with the politicians and how they "fixed people" instead of fixing problems and processes.

As a teacher of MBA students, my students were not interested in my past first career but they were serious about how they can do well and get good score in the examination, how they can get good jobs and how they can face interview and how they can manage their eccentric and irritant bosses. The biggest challenge in a second career is to share one's experience and professional knowledge in such a way that it fits into the present problems and context. Very often the old will sermonize out of context and the young will switch off their antennas! Management education, unlike other types of education is all about getting results and finding. If the elderly and senior teacher does not give solutions then they are not valued by the students.

In my second Career as a Teacher I learnt that students are my customers and if the customers are not satisfied then there is something wrong with the teacher's way of imparting and disseminating knowledge. There is a tendency among our faculty in Indian eucational institutions to blame students for the ills of the teacher, the curriculum and the pedagogy. We very often hear that students are useless, they do not read and do not do home work do not concentrate etc. That is precisely the reason why they have come to study and if the Teacher cannot inspire and motivate then that teacher has failed.

For those who want to pursue a second career in the evening of their lives one has to become tech savvy. Internet is now the biggest technology and if the seniors are not conversant with this technology, then whatever second career jobs they take up they will not be able to do their best. As a teacher in my second career I had to learn to browse Wikipedia-the biggest online Encyclopedia and get updated on HRM as an emerging management discipline to be shared with the students in the class room. Books become outdated fast and the periodicals, journals and websites are the ones which remain current. The students get latest emerging thoughts from experts in the field. That way the seniors pursuing the second career are admired and adorned. The final thought that I wish to leave is that if the seniors wish to pursue a second career they have to strengthen their domain knowledge and expertise by whatever methods and means. Without domain knowledge the Seniors cannot enter the job market in the present global world.

Angry Youth vs Corrupt Old

The Leadership crisis in the Middle East, Syria and in India, is all about the angry youth rebelling against the old and corrupt leaders who have not delivered their promised jobs, but amassed wealth for themselves and their kith. Most of these leaders who govern the nation are in the midnight of their lives and are not able to leave a legacy of ethical governance for the good of the nation and their people. The youth everywhere are restless for jobs and livelihood, for education and skills upgradation and for a better quality of life. As per the latest Census of 2011 in India, the youth power is going to be powerful and dangerous particularly in the urban areas as was seen by the Anna Hazare phenomenon.

Revolt in Egypt was all by the 'Youth Bulge' consisting of highly educated youth who were angry and poor. Under six decades of quasi military rule, its old politicians and military officers enjoyed perks and wealth that democracy now threatens to withhold. In last July, thousands of unemployed young Spaniards, called *los indignados* (the indignant), protested in cities across Spain and marched to Brussels to draw attention to the high jobless rate of 40 per cent. *The Economists* special report on The Future of Jobs' is revealing a global discontent of the youth which may trigger more dangerous political events.

According to the Mckinsey Global Institute, three types of jobs are created now all over the world (1) Transformational (construction jobs), (2) Transactional (such as routine jobs in banks, secretarial / clerical work for bosses), and (3) Interactional (knowledge work, collaboration with others, management consultancy, high skilled technology jobs). The transformational work has come down in the west, but steamrolls in China and India. The policy makers-politicians-most of them being old in India and other countries, don't understand the complexities of global job creation and tend to devote more on transformational (infrastructure and construction jobs where- they also get some cuts).

In the big cities of the world where the new rich young couple work and have dependant parents, the demand for homecare workers is great. America alone will need two million more of them in the next decade. But homecare service is not a flagship job and as we see more of the educated youth emerging in India, they prefer the interactional jobs.

Most of our graduates in technology and management, though good in their academic accomplishments, are found by many Companies who hire them as not 'employable'. *Infosys* in India spends a lot of time and money to make them employable even after they are recruited. This means, what we teach in the classrooms are not relevant to those who employ the graduates and this calls for a relevant syllabus and employable skills to be taught.

Statues as Solution for Starvation?

I was recently in Lucknow, and UP has a Chief Minister known for slogans to catch the minds of the poverty-stricken youth. Crores are spent to build pink stone structures and statues of late Dr. Bhimrao Ambedakar, Kanshi Ram and Buddha as well as huge stone structures without any shady trees in the heart of Lucknow. I asked the taxi driver, while driving to the Lucknow Airport along these statues and parks, how these huge gardens without trees and redstone walls help the citizens of Lucknow and the people of UP? His answer was really smart: "Sir, instead of these monstrosities, the CM should have established more industries and factories around Lucknow to help the dalits and the educated poor to get jobs and lead productive lives. Instead, she is helping the builders and contractors of such useless statues!" In his own style, he asked me how these corrupt politicians of the country can be taught lessons in job creation for the young workforce? The slogan of the UP CM, *Sarvajan hitay and Sarva jana sukhay,* can be turned in the words of my taxi driver into *'Netas hitay and Contractors sukhay!*

As I travel around the world, I find the young have developed a hatred for the elderly corrupt leaders. The Italian Prime Minister Silvio Berlusconi's trial on sex charges, at 70 plus, is a disgrace to a nation known for culture and civilisation. How can the old attract the young by their ethical leadership qualities? That is the million dollar question of this century.

Conflict of Culture

Raise your voice against the abuses on children and women in the name of rituals.

Despite decades of medical advances in the US, doctors are

still faced with many a dilemma on treating the general public. The cultural practices in some countries are atrocious and cannot be justified on any moral or health grounds, but continue to the detriment of people and society. Female circumcision is one such, dangerous and criminal, but still practised in many African and Islamic countries. The religious heads, who are not medical experts, support these practices in the name of preserving particular religious practice and culture. The American Academy of Pediatrics (AAP), in a review of its policy on the practice of female circumcision, first allowed its doctors to perform some kind of 'ritual cut' in the clitoral skin to satisfy the cultural requirement of people wedded to the practice of female circumcision. *(The Economist,* June 12, 2010)

But suddenly, when many paediatricians opposed even this ritual cut, President Judith Palfrey withdrew this mandate and vehemently opposed all forms of genital cutting on girls. The AAP is a professional body, which should not have allowed such practices in the first place, to be reversed later in the face of opposition. These professional bodies should not become lobbyists, but should retain their scientific culture to promote the best interests of the patents or the public whom they serve (in this case, the girl child). No laws exist against male circumcision in any Western country. No records are kept of circumcisions performed outside the hospitals and there is no regulation of ritual practitioners. Some doctors in the West feel that male circumcision is helpful in slowing the spread of HIV/AIDS. Here again we find a sexual bias among the professionals!

Ritual Abuse vs Medical Ethics

The World Health Organization (WHO) estimates that 100-140 million women have been subject to such practices and 3 million girls are at risk each year of one of the four forms of cutting — ranging from the symbolic to life ruining. In countries such as Somalia, Egypt and Guinea, over 95 per cent of women have undergone some version of it. Nearly 18 African countries have banned these practices, although laws are patchily observed. In Indonesia, an Islamic country, the ban is effective, notes WHO, basically because of female education and empowerment.

Even in India, data on female circumcision is not forthcoming because of fear of the clergy. In UP and Bihar, some religious groups are promoting female circumcision in a clandestine fashion. Thus the girl children in India are also exposed to this practice, along with child marriage, child sex abuse, child prostitution and many such types of child abuse.

Nicholas Christof and Sheryl WuDunn, the Pulitzer Prize winners, in their latest book, *Half the Sky,* have narrated with live examples how girls and women have made a difference to their own abused lives and the lives of girls and women, despite the havoc played on them by men/husbands and the so called 'Sugar Daddies' (elderly men abusing young girls)! Honour killings and Khap Panchyats are a disgrace to India's freedom and the sooner we attack these, the better it is for our girls, women and mothers. (All mothers are women, but not all women are mothers!)

The latest trend in India in the abuse of females, and deprived women in general, is what has come to be known as 'pregnancy outsourcing'. Childless couples and singles from the US, Europe and South East Asia are looking towards India with the hope of becoming parents. This is all because of money for the poverty-stricken women, where a surrogate mother can get as much as Rs. 3-5 lakhs depending on the paying capacity of the childless couple! This is another type of medical tourism and needs to be regulated to save our girls and young mothers from all types of abuse.

Where is My School?

Karnataka, and maybe most other parts of the country, is witnessing rapid closures of government primary schools for want of students or teachers. Is that a good move?

Why's there no drinking water or toilets in my school?"

"My teacher is using the cycle I got from the Government!"

"The noon meals in school are cold and tasteless!"

"My teacher says the school will be closed because we are only 5 students."

These were the questions raised by six year old kids when the Chief Minister of Karnataka held the Children's Day interactive session on 14th November 2011.

After a series of scandals, the current Karnataka Government is inviting disgrace to itself by closing around 1,500 primary schools on the ground they have less than five children and hence uneconomical for the State Primary Education department to manage them. Primary Education is not a business, and under the Right to Education Act, even if there is one child, that child has a right to attend a primary school and it is the duty of the State to provide the learning space for the child.

Merger is the Answer

So it is high time the leaders of this government learn how to govern with a 'human face' in their remaining tenure. The biggest human face in the State is that of a child, and children have to be provided with the learning space in their own village and not walk hours to attend a school. The Minister of the State Primary Education says the State will provide autos for those kids dislodged from the school who cannot walk long distances to attend other primary schools, and this smacks of any commonsense. Rural schools are not like urban schools, and walking to the school cutting across tanks, shrubs and green fields is itself a learning experience.

There are four critical factors for a growing child below 10 years to learn:

- the parents who have to send the child to school
- the teacher who makes learning fun and interesting
- an attractive and comfortable school building, and
- learning materials like books, slates and chalk pieces.

Among these four, the teacher plays a critical role to attract kids to the schools. In Karnataka, a primary school teacher in a rural area gets as much as Rs. 20,000 per annum. Most of them loiter ground without teaching, and are busy in running grocery and tea shops in the village. Why can't the Karnataka Government dismiss them and merge the schools with less children to the preschools called *Anganwadis,* where kids in the age group of 3-5 attend, and where nutritional supplements are also provided? *Anganwadis* are run by the Social Welfare Department and the Primary Schools are run by the Education Department, and there is no coordination between them.

At present, kids between age 3-5 go to *Anganwadis,* and then enter primary schools at 6 plus, and high schools at 14 plus. When the *Anganwadis* were established across the country, the idea was to prepare the kids to go to primary school without dropping out. Now the primary schools with fewer kids can be merged with the *Anganwadis* and this integration will be more useful and productive, instead of closing them. This will be like merging in terms of space, and not in terms of learning. Another alternative would be to outsource these schools to private teachers or institutions who should run them instead of closing them. I hope better sense prevails with the political leaders in Karnataka on such critical issues affecting the children of the State.

The Ernst and Young Story

It was a bright evening on 23rd June in the Marriott Hotel in the suburb of New Jersey in the US when my wife and I were invited to witness the gala dine and wine event of the flagship firm, Ernst and Young—a 100-year old company in the US, specialising in finance, entrepreneurship and management consultancy. The event was to honour the entrepreneurs who have made a difference in the US, in innovation and wealth creation. For the last 25 years, Ernst and Young has been providing this enthusiasm, passion and inspiration for entrepreneurs in 140 cities and 50 countries worldwide. Some 30 entrepreneurs were honoured in New Jersey on that day, among them three Indians who were honoured for their outstanding work in the fields of Information Technology, Pharmaceuticals and Software solutions. Some Americans were honoured for many interesting ventures — Buddy Valastro won the Award for preparing and selling Red Velvet Cakes and Signature flower cupcakes! The role of the entrepreneur has never been more vital than it is today, not just in the US but all over the globe. Indian entrepreneurs in the US have made an impact not just in the Silicon Valley, but also in different regions of the US.

Winners All!

Eight category winners were announced from a pool of 37 finalists representing 28 companies. A few outstanding Indian Entrepreneurs honoured were:

Sunil Mehta, who founded *The Orion Systems Integrators* in 1993 single-handed, which is a one stop-shop for all computer and IT needs. He also built an ERP Supply Chain product for the retail industry.

The two brothers, Chintu Patel and Chirag Patel, are founders of *Amneal Pharmaceuticals*—a fast-growing generic pharmaceutical company in the US - and have achieved remarkable results in the fields of dermatology, biologicals, and breakthrough oxygenation therapy. They are making a difference to the way healthcare is provided in America.

The third finalist was Jay Kulkarni, who founded *Theorem* in 2002 using his own savings, to provide specialised services to the internet Advertisement Companies. *Theorem* is now servicing more than 150 clients around the world. Jay built *Theorem* through customer service, quality execution and a highly motivated team. It has opened a London office to support the European market, providing a multilingual account management staff, and established a Dominican Republic operation as a competitive Latin American base.

Indian entrepreneurs are now driving the US economy which is undergoing a recession of high magnitude. Ernst and Young's Strategic Growth Forum, held every year for the Global Entrepreneurs, is the world's leading venue for entrepreneurs striving for success, as well as for those individuals whose companies are established market leaders and want to keep growing and going. They also honours women who are now emerging worldwide, in their own right as powerful leaders and entrepreneurs.

Two Freedom Struggles and One Life

In the wake of globalisation and growing crony capitalism in India, there is an urgent need for our young generation to get a glimpse of how in the early days of freedom struggle our leaders, with intellectual capital and patriotic passion, handled the worst refugee problems in the wake of India's freedom, how the concern for people was at the top of the political agenda of the Congress, and how the same Congress over the years has degenerated into a party of cronies and sycophants.

Laxmi Chand Jain, who passed away recently, was a great rebel and an ardent lover of grassroots activism and development. His book, Civil *Disobedience* : *Two Freedom Struggles* and *One Life* reads like a textbook for management students who wish to understand how people problems can be managed both in peace and troubled situations. Born to a freedom fighter and business family of Rajasthan, L.C. Jain was never attracted to business or a cushy job, and his entire life was a mission for inclusive growth and human development, based on Gandhian values. Married to a feminist activist and an Oxford Graduate and one time teacher in Miranda House of Delhi University, the story of Laxmi and Devaki is best captured in the Chapter called Thirty Rupee Wedding[1]!

A Grassroots Gandhian

Chandni Chowk in Delhi is known for Marwari business families, Muslim, retailers, and Biriyani restaurants surviving side by side and engaged in thriving business. In the wake of India's Freedom and the birth of Pakistan, 1947 saw the worst massacre of Hindus and their flight to Delhi from Lahore, Multan and Bhawalpur, and Kingsway Camp was the biggest refugee camp. As many as 10,000 refugees-consisting of children, who lost their education, old men and women-were to be consoled, and Jain left his studies and joined the 500 young volunteer brigade to help them emotionally and physically in the Free India. Some of the refugees were shouting against Gandhi, saying he sold out to Muslims by agreeing to the division of India. Against such high tempers and emotional outbursts, Jain jumped into the most difficult task of settling them with livelihoods, and not just feeding them.

The most revealing facet of this book is how as a Grassroots Gandhian, L.C. Jain, inspired by leaders like Kamala Devi Chattopadhyaya, could shock the bigwigs in New Delhi like Sir

Datar Singh, Advisor in the then Ministry of Agriculture, who was allotted 3000 acres of land left behind by the Muslims who migrated to Pakistan. Similarly, M.S. Randhwa, the then Dy Commissioner of Delhi, was allotted 600 acres and M.S. Sahni, Principal of Law College in Delhi, was allotted 1200 acres. Getting these lands allotted for the refugees from Pakistan, divesting them from the bigwigs, and make them cultivate under the cooperative farming arrangement, was not an easy task.

The Central Government bureaucrats were hostile to the whole idea of cancelling these land grants to big guns, and then allotting them to refugees for cultivation. L.C. Jain persuaded the refugees to move to occupy these lands in the village of Chattarpur in Mehrauli near Delhi, and start cultivation. Till the harvest, they were provided ration to live and work. Senior Congress leaders like Pandit Nehru supported this move, and thus we could see the integrity of the then Congress leaders. Nehru wrote to the then Home Minister, Sardar Vallabhbhai Patel: "Someone told me these land allotments to these officers were made in exchange for land in Pakistan. This does not seem to be sufficient justification. When land is so scarce and so many unfortunate people need it, it seems unfair that large slices of it be given to our officers." This is the difference between our earlier great leaders and the present day leaders of all parties, who want to grab the scarce land on all filthy pretexts for their kith and kin. The Indian Cooperative Union (ICU), about which Jain had a great regard, took the initiative and moved the refugees to Chattarpur and started cooperative farms.

Even today if someone knows about the New Delhi land mafia and how the farmhouse phenomenon works, we could imagine how difficult it was for people like Jain to work with corrupt bureaucracy and the Ministers of those days. Even Indira Gandhi had a farmhouse in Chattarpur, and Sanjay Gandhi had a tough time with Jain when the Emergency was declared.

Jain's other landmark achievements were the scaling up of handicrafts and handlooms in India. The present nationwide sale and exhibition of handlooms, handicrafts and cottage industry products was the outcome of the early efforts of people like Kamla Devi Chattopadhyaya and L.C. Jain. Grassroots Gandhism has come to stay, but where are the leaders like L.C. Jain who can provide that VIM (Vision, Inspiration and Momentum)?

The Golden Years of IIM in Ahmedabad

Ahmedabad city in Gujarat was known as a textile city in the sixties, and these highly mechanised industries survived along with Mahatma Gandhi's *charkha,* a symbol of 'human labour'. The city was also known for the illustrious families of Sarabhais and Lalbhais who staunchly supported the Mahatma in his non-violent struggle against the British for India's Independence.

It was in 1960 the Space Scientist Dr. Vikram Sarabhai returned from his Cambridge course and settled in Ahmedabad to convert the city currently known for its flagship management education and Physical Science Research—two different fields altogether. The traditional business tycoons of Ahmedabad laughed at his idea because they thought management cannot be taught, and managers and entrepreneurs are born and not made! Dr. Sarabhai, known for his radical ideas and passion for institution-building, took upon this challenge of establishing this great Institution known worldwide as the Indian Institute of Management, Ahmedabad (IIMA), which launched its Golden Jubilee Celebrations in December 2010. This yearlong festival will be known for its innovations, new areas of management education and research, and programmes to bring in a new spirit to its growing glory for India.

My Connection

I was privileged to work in this Institution as a Visiting Faculty in its Centre for Management in Agriculture (CMA) during 1974-76. It goes to the vision of its founders and all its Directors to remember its faculty and staff who served over the years, to invite them and honour them with a Shawl and a Plaque, and listen to their reminiscences and develop a strategy for its growth for the next 50 years. The current Director, Prof Samir Barua, and the Dean of its Alumni Activities, Dr. Atanu Ghosh, and the entire staff and student community managed the event with precision and great affection. Mrinalini Sarabhai, well-known dancer and wife of Dr. Vikram Sarabhai, was the Chief Guest.

The first event was the demonstration of a 'domino effect', clicked off by Prof. Barua, and made by the students of IIMA to break the Microsoft Record and Limca Book of Records of 7,000 dominoes. They used 11,000 dominoes to create the Golden Jubilee Logo, and these dominoes were made of compressed sawdust and not the regular wooden ones. There was also a brainstorming session of the present Faculty with the former ones, chaired by Prof. Barua, who provided a glimpse of what the DMA did in the last five decades and how it has emerged as a Global Institute for Management Education, not just in India but in the whole of Asia. According to the ranking by the reputed EQUIS - a rating agency for management institutes in the World- IIMA is now No 5 in the world for its excellence in management education. Sixty per cent of the current Indian CEOs are IIMA alumni. Apart from its two-year post graduate programme (PGP), the IIMA has branched off in several areas of concern to the corporate sector through its training, consultancy and research activities. It has centres for innovation, incubation and entrepreneurship, for management in agriculture, for infrastructure policy and regulation, for retailing, for insurance, and finally an international management group to invite the best of Management students to spend time in the IIMA.

One Man's Vision

The unique work done by the IIMA was initiated by its founder Dr Vikram Sarabhai, who was a Cambridge-trained Space Scientist and was persuaded to be the Head of Atomic Energy by our first Prime Minister, Pandit Jawaharlal Nehru. But his passion to build'a world-class management institute could not be contained. He collaborated with the Harvard Business School to train the Faculty of the IIMA in the initial years, and invited the world-renowned French Architect, Louis Kahn, to build the 'brick precincts' for training the future entrepreneurs and managers of emerging India.

Dr. Sarabhai always believed in leadership succession and passed on the baton to Prof. Ravi Mathai, another visionary and not just a Management Guru. Late Prof. Mathai was known for his radical views, ranging from corporate ethics to public affairs. He stepped down as Director after a five-year stint, and set the precedent that all Directors step down every five years, even now followed in the IIMA. The greatest contribution of Prof. Mathai was to develop rural entrepreneurs like artisans, craftsmen and women leather workers and many village enterprises. Even after three decades, the leather workers of Jaweja in Rajasthan, whose skills Prof. Mathai supported, are booming with their exportable leather products like footwears and handbags.

The IIMA has done enough in the last five decades to promote 'Talentship' of the corporate world, but has done nothing to build the Public Leadership in the country. It has to move from talentship to leadership - not just in the Indian corporate world, but in the entire country. Look at the scams promoted by our leaders (politicians) in the country. Institutions like IIMA cannot remain as silent spectators. There is a need to set up a Centre for Leadership Development in IIMA and engage in building a leadership pipeline for our country from Gram

Sabha to Vidhan Sabha to Lok Sabha and Rajya Sabha. God bless IIMA!

The Anna Hazare Phenomenon

India can easily be turned into a benevolent State if all our leaders adhere to good governance.

Many middle class families in the Metros, sipping wine or beer, keep talking mostly in their drawing rooms on corruption and how our MBA—Ministers, Businessmen and Administrators — nexus has landed this country in a mess. Thanks to Anna Hazare, they moved to Jantar Mantar this time and joined him in a campaign to clean this country from corruption and nepotism and move forward in the 21st century.

We have three public opinion-making streams in this country, shaped by civil society groups led by people like Anna Hazare - the bureaucrats, politicians and the business tycoons. Unless we break this nexus, civil society groups can only keep on shouting and fasting in Jantar Mantar and nothing is going to happen. How will we clean this MBA nexus and build a class of new leaders from the bottom up to carry the VIM - vision, inspiration and momentum—of this country, generated by thousands of passionate people who are not in its direct governance? One Lok Pal Bill will not help, unless the electoral politics is cleaned up and we get honest and passionate leaders in our legislatures, from the Gram Sabhas right up to the Vidhan Sabhas and Lok Sabha, to frame policies affecting the citizens of India. This one man or woman or a group of men and women Lok Pal, despite the rigorous selection through judicial and political processes, can be a Frankenstein who can be vindictive and eccentric and also corrupt! If the Lok Pal is beyond scrutiny by the Parliament or the Judiciary, the consequences can be even more dangerous and frightening.

Join the System

Our Parliament is now a madhouse of elected representatives, half of them tainted with criminal background. How can we expect any VIM from them? If we can make our electoral politics and our representative democracy more transparent and open, and make the MPs, MLAs and Panchayat Pradhans more professional and honest, our policies and processes will also be transparent and people-friendly. Why not the civil society conscience-keepers get into these elected bodies and shout, instead of shouting from the Jantar Mantar? Let them fast in the Central Hall of Parliament instead of Jantar Mantar! Even the Civil Society is divided just not on Lok Pal Bill but on many other issues of national governance.

There are three types of Civil Societies or NGOs. First are those who carry laptops and are found in airports, hobnobbing with ministers and business tycoons and fund-givers to get funds for their activities and are good in making glamorous reports and Power Point presentations. They are also called advocacy NGOs, talking mostly on public issues. But they are far removed from the grassroots, The other types are those who struggle in forests and tribal areas to help the tribal poor. Some of these have been dubbed as Maoists. They are called grassroots activists, who invoke the Right to Information Act and harass innocent officials to get information on frivolous issues affecting individuals.

In this Anna Hazare episode of good intentions, there are some like Sanjaya Baru, the Editor of *Business Standard* and former Media Advisor to Dr. Manmohan Singh, who called this a 'Hazare Hazard'! Some activist groups like National Campaign for People's Right to Information (NCPRI), headed by Aruna Roy, Shekar Singh, and Harsh Mandar, are opposed to the Anna Hazare group proposing a Lok Pal Bill. Like political rivals, civil society groups are also divided. Then how will the ordinary public believe in them? It is all media hype which has given these activists a big mileage, and media has also become a *tamasha* for the public to enjoy and forget these events.

The Singapore Model

Can the State then be a saviour of citizens? Unfortunately, the State is managed by politicians through democratic participation, and they have lost their balance of judgement and concern for the citizens. They don't want the electoral laws to be changed to allow honest citizens to get into Assemblies or Parliament. For the common men and women, boys and girls in India, the distinction between the 'political' and the 'economic', the 'public' and the 'private', is getting blurred. Business and politics are closely intertwined-indeed politics is also a form of business, a lucrative one indeed! Politics-as-business and business-as-politics runs deep in the Indian psyche today. How can our one billion people trust our State as 'human', 'efficient', and 'protective' of their rights and livelihoods? This is the crux of the problem of governance by the State.

Today Singapore, a tiny State in the East, is one of the best governed State in the World. Singapore beckons - 'Come to us, and you will get excellent infrastructure, educated workforce, open trade routes, the rule of law, and low taxes'. Singapore's competitive advantage has been a good and less costly government. It has worked hard to keep its State small. There are no freebies as we have in India like free TVs and free ration. In the words of Lee Kuan, the great founder-leader of Singapore, "Singapore is not a free lunch welfare State!" Any State can be turned into a benevolent one if all our leaders carry on their VIM to make India great. The earlier the civil society activists and the corporate world realise this, the better it is for the citizens of India!

The 'Milk Man' of India : The Untold Story

A tribute to Dr. Verghese Kurien, who raised India to the top of the world in milk production with his 'white revolution'.

The sad demise of Dr. Verghese Kurien, the Milk Man of India, has brought to the fore the leadership qualities of entrepreneurship and management skills of those who want to make the farm sector in India a global feature of Indian economy. Unfortunately, the present political and corporate leaders in India will never learn and build on the passions of such great leaders and visionaries. In the 40s when he returned from studies abroad, it was late Sardar Vallabhbhai Patel who spotted him in Anand and inspired him to stay put, despite the many tempting offers Dr. Kurien get for his talent and personality.

Many farmers of Gujarat in the undivided Bombay State in the 40s used to sell their milk travelling all the way to Bombay suburban area where *Polson* butter and milk products were made. The great visionary Sardar Patel asked a simple question to Dr. Kurien: "Why not our farmers and their women, who milk their cows and buffaloes, sell their milk here only in Anand? How can a milk processing plant of the *Polson* type be built in Anand so that the Gujarat farmers, and Anand farmers in particular, get benefits of a good price for their milk?" This was the beginning of a long 'Milk journey' of not only Dr. Kurien but also the entire farming women and men of Anand.

In the 50s and 60s, Pandit Nehru, the first Prime Minister of India, and Sardar Patel, a powerful Home Minister of India, were the visionary leaders, and the cooperative movement was in its infancy. Sugar cooperatives were organised to get better price for sugarcane growers. Farmers' credit cooperatives were also formed despite their bad performance in credit management. The Reserve Bank of India once said in the 60s: "The Cooperative Movement has failed, but it must succeed".

The women of Kaira District were the ones who really managed their cows and buffaloes and earned their income from the sale of milk. The middlemen who bought their milk exploited them by giving them less price on the ground of low fat content and other imaginary quality ctoubts. All this was carefully assessed by Dr. Kurien by his tireless field visits, observing how the women were exploited by middlemen and hoteliers who buy their milk.

'Operation Flood'

Milk cooperatives were thus formed in Kaira District and the first milk pasteurising plant was donated by UNICEF in 1948 or so. Dr. Kurien was a keen observer of minute details linked with the health of cows/buffaloes, how women struggle to bring milk to the collection centres, how they should know the fat content of their milk to get a better price, and how to improve the health of the milch cattle, their artificial insemination, and so on, to improve the milk yield. The women who brought milk to the collection centres both in the morning and evening were paid on the spot, based on the fat content of the milk they bring. They were taught how to measure the fat content. The Kaira District Milk Cooperatives were formed and Anand became the headquarters of the pasteurising plant and thus emerged the Anand Milk Union Ltd. (AMUL) - a federation of several village level milk cooperatives and now claims 35 lakhs of milk producers!

It was Tribhuvandas Patel as head of Kaira District Milk Producers Union who supported Dr. Kurien to build the scientific supply chain of milk from the bottom, upto pasteurising and so on into different milk products, branding them etc. When Pandit Nehru died, Lal Bahadur Shastri became the Prime Minister. He had heard a lot about the Gujarat Milk Unions and the success story of *Amul.* He came down to Kaira District and stayed in a village and observed the entire process of milk collection by women. Shastri asked Kurien, "Can you replicate this model all over India?" "Yes, but I will do it sitting in Anand and not in Krishi Bhavan of New Delhi!!" Shastri agreed, and thus the National Dairy Development Board (NDDB) was bom and stationed in Anand, and not in Delhi. The rest is now a known story.

When *Amul* milk powder was brought to the market, mothers started bottle-feeding their infants, instead of breast-feeding. When the UNICEF India Country Head in the 80s told Dr. Kurien not to produce milk powder which promotes bottle-feeding and substitutes mother's milk, he bluntly told UNICEF not to interfere in his business! Dr. Kurien was eccentric, humorous, blunt and could go to any extremes to attain his goals, which were generally inclusive of the "farm men/women at large". As head of the NDDB, he sent 50 buffaloes to the King of Thailand to commemorate 50 years of his rule, by an Air India charter flight. Questions were asked, "What happens when they urinate in the flight and fight and break the aircraft?" Dr. Kurien said, "We will sedate them and will not feed them, and the buffaloes will enjoy the flight!"

"I Had a Dream"

Dr. Kurien was an institution builder, and despite the premier Indian Institute of Management at Ahmedabad being just a few miles away from Anand, he said managing buffaloes and cows and getting value from them for village women is a different ball game, and not for the Harvard-collaborated NM. He set up the now famous and 35 year old Institute of Rural Management at Anand, whose graduates are now placed in many multinational food conglomerates around the world.

'Operation Flood took India from being a milk-deficient nation, to the largest milk producer in the world, surpassing the USA in 1998, with about 17 per cent of global output in

2010-11, which in 30 years doubled the milk available to every person. Dairy farming became India's largest self-sustaining industry. He made the country self-sufficient in edible oils too later on, taking head-on the powerful and entrenched oil supplying lobby, with *Dhara*.

All States in India have now their Sate level Milk Federations and Karnataka boasts of a well-managed Federation that sell milk products under the brand name 'Nandini'. But the women who bring milk to the collection centres are not paid on the same day. The best tribute the Federation can pay to Dr. Kurien is to respect these women by paying them on the same day, both morning and evening.

One of the greatest proponents of the cooperative movement in the world, Dr. Kurien's work has alleviated millions out of poverty, not only in India but also outside. Hailed as the "Milkman of India", Kurien won several awards including the Padma Vibhushan (India's second highest civilian honour), the World Food Prize and the Magsaysay Award for community leadership.

Corporate Ethics: Preaching or Practising?

I once put in a general question to my students of an MBA Class, whether corporate ethics is only for preaching or for practising. A smart girl answered, "Sir, preaching is easy and practising is difficult." I asked 'why?, and a boy answered, "Sir, because practising involves a lot of personal difficulties, inconvenience, patience in telling others why one does not like to give bribe or take bribe etc., etc., and the best way is to take bribe, keep quiet and keep on moving !!"

This is what exactly is happening in the corporate world and in our country's governance, at all levels form Panchayats to the National Parliament. Many corporate leaders around the world are caught up in many scandals. Rajat Gupta in the US, a former Director of Goldman Sachs, McKinsey and what have you, is on trial in the US for insider trading. Late Dr. Madhav Mehra, Founder of World Council for Corporate Governance in London, was a great champion of the need for ethical Corporate Directors to be on Corporate Boards. In his Master Class for Directors, which he ran for many years in India, he was always hitting on ethical values in the Management of Corporate Boards than on complicated management of financial dealings to save oneself from being caught. I once asked him in one of the Master Class why highly-educated Harvard-trained corporate executives go so low as to be caught up in financial scandals? He said, "In big Ivy League Business Schools, they teach HNGC (How Not To Get Caught) and HLSTO (How to Look smarter than Others)!!"

Integrity Management

It is just not corporate honchos who are caught up in many scandals. Many iconic sportsmen have been exposed in many unethical practices. *The New York Times* recently carried a feature on how Lance Armstrong has been shown unethical in using performance-enhancing drugs during the seven years when he won the *Tour De France.* During the same period, Armstrong started 'Livestrong' - a cancer-suport organisation known for its ubiquitous yellow bracelets. The question raised is, is the unethical nature of Lance's doping offset by the fact that his Livestrong Organisation has touched many lives in a positive way?' Even Rajat Gupta was a great philanthropist and founded many Institutions like the Indian School of Business in Hyderabad and a man like Bill Gates pleaded before the US Judiciary to condone the lapses of Gupta.

You cannot engage in unethical practice from the left hand and do good by the right hand. This is where the 'means and ends' become important. Mahatma Gandhi, in his *Experiments with Truth,* always believed in ethical means even if the ends are not achieved. Today corporate leaders keep talking all the time on Philanthropy and Corporate Social Responsibility, which is now made mandatory to spend 2 per cent of the corporate enterprise profits in the recently amended Company's Act, 1956.

Philanthropy is easier to practise than engage in CSR because giving a cheque is easier than getting involved in improving a situation or helping a group of people or an organisation. Philanthropy is described by a Harvard Management expert as 'an arm's length charity - just issue a cheque to a needy man or a woman or an organisation and just forget.

Banks and financial institutions also need to practise ethical dealings, which is not happening at present. Tax havens and offshore financial centres are now much sought out by the wealthy to avoid taxes by engaging in unethical practices. Smart lawyers and accountants advise on how to avoid taxes and keep them in tax havens. Santa Claus is being booed for living offshore!

According to *The Economist,* elites of 139 low-middle income countries like India, Pakistan and some African countries have parked up to $ 9.3 trillion of unrecorded wealth offshore! No amount of regulation would bring back this wealth to the home countries and our Indian corporate honchos and politicians are happy to keep their 'Laxmi' in those offshore havens!!

5

Good Governance for Survival and Living

Does Mahatma Gandhi Matter Anymore?

The Hind Swaraj is now being revisited and many Centenary International Seminars and discussions are being held under the auspices of think-tanks like the Council for Social Development, New Delhi. Many of the social and economic issues Mahtama Gandhi thought and acted on after he wrote in the *Hind Swaraj*— peace and world order, feminism and swaraj, religion and social imagination — are now being discussed because these are still burning issues. In the *Hind Swaraj,* we do get a glimpse of what Gandhi thought about technologies to empower the rural poor of India in the twenties and thirties, (Anthony J. Parel- "Gandhi and Hind Swaraj" and other writings, Cambridge University Press, 1997).

Gandhi said: "I discovered the wheel in London in 1909, and we had many long conversations about the condition of India with students and earnest Indians. And I saw in a flash that without the spinning wheel there was no swaraj. I knew at once everyone had to spin. I didn't know when, I didn't know the distinction between the loom and the wheel, and in *Hind Swaraj* I used the word loom to mean the wheel."

In his *Autobiography,* Gandhi has elaborated extensively about the Charkha: "In Sabarmati Satyagraha Ashram, our objective was to clothe ourselves entirely in cloth manufactured by our own hands. This enabled us to know from direct experience the conditions of life among the weavers, the extent of their production, how they get yarn supply, how they were cheated by the mills producing yarn, and their growing indebtedness. It was Gangaben who found the spinning wheel in Vijapur in Baroda State.

Wheeling in Freedom

Charkha was just not a spinning wheel for Mahatma. It emerged as a symbol of self reliance, self-empowerment and self-rule. "Gram Swaraj" was his dream and today we still find the Gram Sabhas relevant, to know what goes on, where and how things happen to the villagers. But these Gram Sabhas are never held under one pretext or the other despite a Constitutional provision to hold them.

If Gandhi was alive, how would he have reacted to the emerging technologies affecting the rural poor? What technologies would he have preferred to empower rural artisans like carpenters, masons, self-employed women and men? Is charkha still relevant in the 21st century 'developing' India with its 70 per cent of the population still dependent on agriculture and farming? What would Gandhi have thought of the computer that revolutionalises the way we live, connect with our neighbours, get information, and move ahead with the times to make a better living? How would he have reacted to the information revolution helping us become good and responsible citizens, or the technologies disrupting moral values? What would he have preferred and promoted for Gram Swaraj, after achieving Hind Swaraj? Can the chip and charkha survive together in this age of globalisation and unethical corporatisation?

Globalisation is inevitable and unavoidable, and Gandhi would have used global technologies to help the poor and the marginalised. He would have been the first to think and embrace what is now called 'Glocal' - global and the local at the same time.

His biggest dream of promoting Gram Swaraj in India would have been possible with the use of Internet and making the information available to the most vulnerable people in the villages. Despite the 73 Constitutional Amendments, our Panchayats and Gram Sabhas are still in the dark about what goes around in their own village because our Sarkari Yojanas do not converge at the Gram level. If *Bhoomi* in Karnataka can provide digital land records to every villager, why cannot the Government make a Gram Sabha Information System (GSIS) like GIS or GPS and make transparent all the transactions at the village, known to even a village child? Our scientists use digital and satellite pictures in their international conferences, but the average villager does not know what is happening around his/her own village through hundreds of these Yojanas. As a tribute to our Father of the Nation, the Government of India should develop GSIS for all the thousands of Gram Panchayats in the country and promote Gram Swaraj.

Jai Hind!

Corporate Philanthropy, Social Responsibility and Inclusive Growth - Opportunities and Complicities

The recent visit of Warren Buffet and Bill gates to talk of Corporate Philanthropy to the Indian Corporate Leaders has made news and this has raised the expectations of the civil society and a large majority of the policy makers that something great is going to happen to the art and practice of "giving" in India. Over the years Indian Corporate Houses like the Tatas the Birlas and many enterprises have been engaged in building Institutes of higher education and learning and also building Temples by the Hindustan Charities of the Birlas. India has a rich tradition of philanthropy but in the context of global environmental threats and public health issues like the threat of TB, Malaria and HIV/AIDS, our corporate Leaders in India have to rethink on the art and practice of giving for human wellbeing and happiness rather than for tax benefits, photo and media opportunities. The Government of India is trying to make CSR as an obligatory function of the Corporate enterprises which is an unimaginative initiative and leads to more of compliance and complicity than commitment for the human wellbeing.

Indian Philanthropic initiatives have taken many forms and over the decade in the emerging economic buoyancy many corporates in India have floated Social ventures in the field of education (Azim Premji University), water and environment protection (Argyam of Rohini Nilekani) Social Entrepreneurship of Deshpande Foundation (Sandbox approach to Development of North Karnataka) and so many have flowered across the country. Side by side we see around the country corporates grabbing precious lands of the farmers under the garb of PPP projects to build infrastructure and special economic zones (SEZ) . Philanthropy and CSR does not imply giving a cheque from the right hand and taking it away from the left hand as has happened in many tribal areas of Orissa where POSCO and Vedanta are at logger heads with the tribals who refuse to vacate their precious land surface. Setting some symbolic Schools and Hospitals as has happened in Vedanta mining areas is neither

CSR nor Philanthropy. Civil Society groups have dubbed the Niyamgiri Hills in Orissa as Vedantagiri and Khandahar mountain Peak in Orissa as POSCO Peak!

The US is known for Philanthropic foundations like Rockefeller Foundation, Ford Foundation and now the Bill Gates Foundation, which have over several decades have ventured into spreading technology for human wellbeing. Research in High Yielding Variety of grains supported by Rockefeller Foundation in sixties in India and Ford Foundation supporting hundreds of NGOs and Educational Institutions in.

India and south East Asia were noble examples of both philanthropy and CSR. Giving is more easy than hand holding the Civil Society Groups and developing their capacities to manage the social ventures. Most of our Indian Philanthropic Organisations are good in giving a cheque than hand holding them for better outcomes.

Mahatma Gandhi always believed in *ethical Means to justify the ends.* Ends in themselves are not enough and if they are achieved by unethical means the ends are unsustainable .Bill Gates Foundation with all its philanthropy is believed to have supported along with Rockefeller foundation the AGRA initiative -Alliance for Green Revolution in Africa. Monsanto in Gates Clothing is the new theme now in Africa (SEE Dark Side of Giving: Rise of Philanthro-Capitalism, *Economic Times*, 25, March 2011) The $ 23.1 Million investment by Gates Foundation in Monsanto, the world's largest producer of GM seeds is a small example of the trend. The Civil Society activists see this as an agenda for pushing GM crops in Africa. Whether this is true or false time alone will tell. But in the meanwhile Bill Gates Foundation should clarify their stand on such controversial technologies like GM crops.

Bill Gates foundation should clarify also many controversies surrounding their entry into Biotech research. According to Eric Holt-Gimenez, Director of US based Food First-Institute for Food and Development Policy, Bill Gates Foundation 30 per cent of its funds went for promoting and developing GM seeds in 2008. However Bill Gates Foundation has done commendable work in health care, TB and Malaria eradication in Africa but it is struggling to discover the vaccine for HIV/AIDS. In Public Health Bill Gates Foundation has out beaten the WHO and many of its scientists have left WHO to join the Bill Gates Foundation - flight of talent if not funds from WHO !

Public Health is not about five star Hospitals where health care has to be paid for. Public health is all about people's health and wellbeing, which they are entitled as a matter of right and not a favor from the State or the Millionaire Doctors. Here again the Corporates are making money than serving the people. One need not declare a CSR programme as such by a Corporate Entity. Take the example of Stem Cells. "Stem cell clinics promise many disabled that they will walk free. Corporate Cord Blood Banks exploit the market for bio insurance-store your baby's umbilical cord blood for a fee-just in case s/he falls ill with some terrible disease that might be cured through the use of those cells." The picture is one of unethical and unscientific medical practice, false advertising, misrepresentation, and the exploitation of peoples desperation hopes and fears.

The publicity generated by such hype helps business" (See Sandhya Srinivasan, The Wild West of Stem Cell Procedures. Agenda Info change Issue No 20, 2010, Centre for Communication and Development Studies, Pune)

India over the generation has respected what are called "commons" - common grazing lands, forests where forest dwellers and tribals collect grass and minor forest produce for their cattle and for their livelihood, common lakes, ponds and water bodies where the villagers can have access to the water for their cattle and for themselves. These are all now under threat in the wake of globalisation and corporate thirst for land and water. How come the Indian government is not legislating on why, how, when these can be used and not used ? It is here where the corporate ethics and sustainability issues come to the fore. In the words of Management Guru Late Dr. Madhav Mehra sustainability strategy needs transparency. Most of our commons in India are under threat of encroachment by the corporate sector. There was a Lake Development Authority in Bangalore which leased out the best Bangalore Lakes for the glamorous floating restaurants depriving the flora and fauna of the lakes. The activist-Environment Support Group brought the stay from the High Court and stopped the corporate group from using the fascinating lakes.

At one time as students of economics we were told about the tragedy of the commons-where everyone has a right to do anything they liked - leading to the misuse, loss and tragedy. The bottled water companies take large quantities of water from underground aquifer for free, and is not treated as the tragedy of the commons ! It is a super tragedy indeed! Now we have digital commons and we do not know what is awaiting in this!

Some have called this as the tragedy of the market and not the commons. (See David Bollier, Commonwealth, Priceless Wealth, Enclosures of the Commons, Agenda Issue 21, 2011, Centre for Communication and Development Studies, Pune).

There is need therefore to look at the CSR issues more in depth and unravel the complexities and complicities so that the philanthropy, CSR and inclusive growth become a reality in the years to come.

Competitive Politics for Good Governance

Principles of corporate governance can be productively used for the governance of the country too.

Indian politics is undergoing rapid changes and the days of single party rule are over. Coalition politics involving alliances of disparate groups will be the scenario of the future both in Parliament and the state assemblies. Coalitions are a type of competitive politics. Just as competition in a market economy leads to better production and services competitive politics should in theory at least lead to better governance.

Many countries in Asia and Africa will face these types of coalition politics and governance. This is to be viewed in the context of the world trend in competitive business and corporate governance with complex set of roles for global companies who wield enormous power of generating wealth and influencing political power. The largest 100 multinationals' $2,000 billion in foreign assets outstrip the combined GDP of China, India, South Korea, Malaysia, Singapore and Phillipines. The multinationals' power has increased greatly and they have to face many complexities to survive. Similarly political parties have to face various complexities where money and peoples' choice play a crucial role.

People Decide

In competitive politics it is the people who decide the fate of governments and in corporate governance the shareholders decide the fate of CEOs and presidents. Both in competitive politics and corporate governance old men nearing retirement are threatened by young leaders. Michael Waldrop in his book 'Complexity, the Emerging Science at the Edge of Order and Chaos' has explained how this theory of complexity works and makes a strong case for decentralisation and empowerment for competitive advantage of firms. Kelvin Kelly, 'Wired' magazine editor, has listed nine principles to take advantage of the phenomenon: (1) Decentralised operations and networked models only work in the long run, (2) Control from the bottom up, (3) Invest in education, (4) Grow by chunking and build the system in pieces, not all at once, (5) Focus on randomness and unpredictability that leads to progress, (6) Honour errors, look for accidents that are competitive advantages, (7) Pursue no optima; have multiple goals. Have alternative plans, (8) Seek persistent disequilibria. Industry revolutionaries create turbulence to open spaces for their product, (9) Change changes itself. Static or incremental strategies often fail.

Political parties may benefit a great deal and may also be able to deliver "development" if they follow some of these principles. Delivering development to benefit people is not going to be easy and the state need not exactly be run like a corporate structure. But there are certain techniques from the corporate world which have relevance to governance. Let us examine the principle of decentralised operations and networked models. Rajiv Gandhi's biggest gift to this country was his passion to decentralise power to the pan-chayats by making them units of self-government. Mahatma Gandhi dreamt of gram swaraj. India is too vast a country to be governed by a few ministers and bureaucrats sitting in New Delhi and state capitals.

Networked Models

Networked models only survive in the end. If all these gram sabhas and panchayats are property networked we get a shining India. NDA's networking is for power sharing and not for networking the 500,000 villages. Unfortunately the same Congress has not bothered to reiterate the decentralisation mantra in the current election manifesto. Instead it has picked up six pedestrian slogans to win the voters hearts. The Congress calls these unfortunately the six basics of governance — Samajik Sadhbhavana, Yuva Rozgar, Grameen Vikas, Arthik Navotfhan, Manila Sashak-tikaran and Saman Avsar. Most of these are outcomes and not techniques and instruments of governance. What are those strategic choices which will promote Saman Avsar or equal opportunity? How will you give Yuva Rozgar when half the Yuva are illiterate? This is linked to education and empowerment. In corporate governance investing in education is a big step to accelerate your competitive edge in knowledge economy. Education alone can usher a knowledge-driven society and polity. None of the parties has emphasised education lift masses from poverty.

Our politicians are not in the habit of honouring their errors. For instance, not once has Narendra Modi said "sorry" to the Gujarat violence victims. Another principle of the complexity theory is you cannot forecast accurately and you have to have alternative plans. Look at the recurrent drought situation. The only alternative plan the Prime Minister has is to link India's rivers, which has technical complexities. There are better ways, to use the phrase of management guru Gary Hamal, to bring change through a "tornado of innovation". There are no such innovations adopted in government systems.

Let us hope we get a government which means business for helping the people and just not getting votes. Let competitive politics lead to better governance.

Gram Swaraj in Karnataka at Crossroads

Gandhiji's dream of empowering our villagers with Gram Panchayats mostly remains a dream, laments.

Mahatma Gandhi, who travelled across the country on foot/ train/bus (not in helicopters), in the days of freedom struggle, believed that 500,000 and odd Indian villages can only be governed by the effective functioning of Gram Sabhas organised by Gram Panchayats. India is a vast and complex country and cannot be governed by our politicians sitting in New Delhi and State Capitals. He believed in building leadership from the bottom up - from Gram Sabhas to Vidhan Sabhas to Lok Sabha, and not in the reverse manner!

The 3-day Conference of hundreds of Gram Panchayat Members and Presidents from 25 districts, organised by the Panchayat Hakkottaya Andolana in Udupi, was a landmark stock-taking of rural governance through these Gram Panchayats in Karnataka. Karnataka was the first State in India to set up a Model Local Governance system, pioneered by late Ramakrishna Hegde and Nazir Saheb. It became an inspiration for late Rajiv Gandhi to push for the 73rd and 74th Constitutional amendments to empower the local bodies as Constitutional wings of the State, to implement innumerable programmes for human development across the country.

But what has happened in Karnataka and elsewhere is a sad story of the Gram Swarajya turning into a Swarajya for the MLAs and MPs and the local bureaucrats to loot the exchequer in the name of effective local governance, bypassing these constitutional bodies called Gram Panchayats (GPs). One MP in Karnataka has used his Local Area Development Fund to build a Sai Baba Temple in his constituency, instead of using it for roads or water, sanitation and health facilities in Panchayat areas. One could hear in Udupi how the Local MLAs in Karnataka have bypassed these elected GPs in choosing rural works and programmes for the rural poor in connivance with the local contractors, to the detriment of the local panchayat residents. Many schemes such as Ashraya Yojana and Mahatma Gandhi Rural Employment Guarantee Programme have remained virtually as parallel programmes of the State Departments without the involvement of the GPs.

Effective Empowerment a Pipedream?

Many issues were brainstormed by these Panchayat Members and a majority of them were passionate women, eager to make a difference to the rural people and not just remain as 'Panchayat Patnis'i Themes discussed were:

Delegation of three Fs -Functions, Funds and Functionaries from the State to these GPs:

- Empowering and protecting the rights of the tribals in the forest areas of Karnataka.
- Urban Local Bodies and their links with neighbouring GPs.
- Strengthening the GP members through knowledge, information and capacity building.

On all these fronts, Karnataka is lagging behind from the so-called backward States like Jharkhand and Bihar, which are struggling to adopt Information Technology tools to strengthen not just Panchayats but the entire governance system. Karnataka boasts as the IT Capital of the World. But the IT excellence is only confined to the Electronics city of Bengaluru, and has not reached the 5000 and odd GPs and 90,000 and odd GP members. 'Bangalore One' is the best example of e-governance for the benefit of Bengaluru city residents who can pay their electricity, phone and water bills at one stroke instead of running around several departments in the city.

There is a need for Gram Panchayat Service Centres (GPSC) in all Karnataka GPs. 'E-Seva' in Andhra, 'SEETU' in Maharashtra, 'Jeevan' in Delhi, 'LokMitra' in Rajasthan, and 'G-Seva' in Gujarat have all established e-govemance systems for the urban citizens. Why not e-governance for Panchayats to bring transparency and accountability and good governance in rural Karnataka? Why should the rural poor go to several State

Departments to get his electricity and land revenue paid or *khata* extract obtained? Can he or she not get it under one counter in a village panchayat? Why, even after two decades, don't we have information stored in a web-friendly Gram Panchayat at the village level so that everyone can get easy access? Despite the appointment of Panchayat Development Officers (PDOs) to help the GPs, we find many PDOs up in arms with the Panchayat Presidents and Members, which speaks of the failure of the State level Panchayat Department to motivate and empower the GP members and the PDOs.

Information is power and withholding information is super power! Hundreds of Panchayat members in Udupi aired their grievances about not getting the right information on Yojanas of the Centre and the State-who gets what, when and how, under these yojanas. One lady Panchayat Member said in anger, "Many Ashraya houses are built but not occupied, and schools with few children are being closed..."

One hopes the State level leaders in Karnataka, who proclaim to be the champions of good governance, learn from the 'voice' of these GP Members and bring-good governance to the rural people of Karnataka.

Urgently Needed: Social Audit of MPs

It will help avoid people' resting too much faith on extra-constitutional panaceas

In the wake of the Anna euphoria, our elected representatives have been dubbed as corrupt and the Team Anna have painted the parliamentarians and Politicians as criminals, corrupt, liars and gavars (coarse and without finesse), which to say the least is uncivilised. True Gandhians would not have used such language. India has its own constitution and several institutions have been enshrined like the executive, legislature and the judiciary and if they are corrupt then we have to find remedies within the framework of law and the constitution and not resort to extra constitutional remedies.

We have elected representatives from the gram panchayat to the state assemblies and to the lok sabha and rajya sabha. We have about 500 and odd lok abhe members and 5,000-odd state assemblies' members and as many as over one lakh elected panchayat members across the country. Thus, we have a staggering number of roughly 2,15,340 and odd elected representatives in different constitutionally established bodies. Besides we have many other elected bodies like milk federations, sugar cooperatives etc where members are elected to protect farming interests etc. These elected representatives constitute the "core decision group" who determine the content, pace, and the direction of the country's governance process. What are the methods by which their promises and performances are judged? Who assesses their performance? What performance indicators are available to evaluate their work? What are the instruments presently employed for monitoring their work in their respective constituencies? MPs have their own MP Local Area Development Scheme (MPLADS) under which every MP gets as much as Rs. 5 crore per year and no one know how that money is spent. There are rare mementos at bus stops and the likes claiming that the work has been funded by a particular MP under MPLADS. Similarly, huge development funds are given to the MLAs to develop their constituencies and no one knows how that money is spent.

These are some of the issues which citizens in a representative democratic form of government should be concerned with. We are more and more concerned with getting better "Value" to the citizen's franchise. At the end of tenure of every elected representative every citizen, who has exercised his/her franchise, is expected to know the tasks accomplished/not accomplished by the elected representatives. MPs and MLAs have a mix of public domain tasks and they spend more time in their own "personal agendas" than in the public domain. These mixes of tasks do not lend themselves for quantification and easy evaluation and we have yet to see any indicators of performance assessment spelt out by MPs or by their party headquarters. In the absence of a formal mechanism to assess the performance of an MP, voters are to fall back on value judgements, image and visibility of the MP in his/her constituency and personal help rendered (specific relief). Some MPs/MLAs nurse their constituency by frequently visiting the area for official meetings or attending events like marriages and funeral ceremonies.

A time has come, when the image of our MPs and Legislators is going down in the wake of rampant corruption charges hurled at them, some founded and some unfounded, to develop a mechanism or a process by which an informed and objective account of the performance of the MP has to be presented at regular intervals of their five year tenure. This cannot be done purely by the Political Party monitoring device or by sending observers of the Party at the time of election contest because it sans objectivity and takes a party view of the performance of the MP.

Just as we have now a well established Social audit of the flagship Mahatma Gandhi Rural Employment Programme across the country, there is an urgent need to engage in the Social Audit of the performance of our Legislators across the country by well intentioned and untainted public figures at the grassroots . Many civil society activists and the Legislators should come together and set up Social Audit Teams for their constituency to establish credibility. If we can do hundreds of environment audits in many controversial projects, we can definitely do untainted and objective Social Audits of the performance of our MPs/MLAs When our MPs/MLAs get elected, he/she should announce

Social Audit Group drawn from the their constituencies representing cross-section of the Voters like landless labourers, artisans, teachers, voluntary agencies, intellectuals, small traders and all those who constitute the "vote bank" in the constituency. This Social audit group should be free from party affiliation/ loyalty. In the span of five years at least three Social audit reports should be presented to the voters. But the MPs/MLAs should share all the information to this Social audit group-greater the information sharing better the social audits.

Making iTEAR Work Micro credit for Inclusive Growth through Innovation, Transparency, Empowerment, Accountability and Responsibility.

The entire Microfinance sector is under attack and scrutiny from regulators to Bankers to activists to Media and to large section of our rural families this sector unfortunately is gathering cloud Either it should rain heavily and wipe out the entire sector or the cloud should disappear for the good of our rural poor who are in need of microfinance. Way back in the Sixties when I studied Agricultural Economics and Rural livelihoods for my" post graduation degree late Prof. M.L. Dantwala—a veteran economist of the Bombay School of Economics-used to emphasise in the class that agriculture and rural living is a way of life and farming has to be treated as a way of life and not as a business. Unfortunately over the years our policy makers and financial strategists have turned to rural areas to do more business than to promote the livelihoods of the deprived rural families. A typical rural woman-entrepreneur is simultaneously engaged in cooking, feeding her child and the buffaloes, cows, grazing the sheep, drawing water and taking care of her drunkard husband and face the threat of local money lenders from whom her husband has taken consumption loan and the Money lender wants the money back without delay. Our earlier cooperative credit structure failed to lift the poor from poverty traps. In the seventies during the days of Nehruvian Socialism the slogan was "Cooperative movement has failed but it must succeed" In the nineties with opening up of the economy and our love for "market economy" we said good bye to the marginalised sections of our rural society and said they should compete for credit in the market. Liberalisation, Privatisation and Globalisation (LPG) became the mantra of Indian Planning Scenario How can the rural poor compete in the huge Urban Oriented Financial Market for small consumption loans and family-oriented enterprises who have no assets except their hands and legs ! Then came Mohamed Yunus who showed in Bangladesh that rural poor have many intangible assets and he mobilised them for credit without hypothecation of their assets and snowed how they can be lifted from poverty traps with microfinance.

Many Indian Microfinance companies bloomed in this decade and when craze and greed become the main driving force for development then there is bound to be disasters and now the entire Microfinance sector in India is under scrutiny. In the name of illiterate women the unethical CEOs of some Microfinance companies made huge fortunes at the cost of rural families among whom some had to commit suicides because they could not repay the loans. Then came heavy handed Ordinance in A.P. which strangulates the freedom of crazy Microfinance Promoters to behave themselves in promoting the livelihoods of the rural borrowers. Some have criticized this Ordinance and some like.

Vijay Mahajan, the Founder of Basix have even dubbed, the Chief Minister of A.P. having been born in a Money Lending family, is trying to subvert the Microfinance to help the Money Lenders But the behaviour of SKS Founder and its sacked CEO are in no way different from the behaviour of village Money

Lenders. They have lost their image because of their unethical standards of lending to the poor and their coercive methods of recovery, which the Village Money Lenders resort to all the time. It is here where the concept of "I-TEAR" propounded by the Founder of Institute of Directors and World Council for Corporate Governance, London Dr. Madhav Mehra assumes importance. I-TEAR is a very simple concept which stands for Innovation, Transparency, Engagement, Accountability and Responsibility. In this world of corporate complexity and deceit it is more difficult to practice simple virtues than practicing complex corporate governance agenda, which are not understood even by the intelligent shareholders. What we need in rural microfinance sector is more simplicity, honesty, ethics and simple to understand procedures and documents by the rural poor. Rural women in India have shown that they are more ethical and honest than corporate honchos. Rural women know how to engage in multitasking, and enterprise management better than any MBA of a high flying Management Institute in our country.

Much has been written in the last few months on what is wrong with this sector and what can be done to revamp it. In all this maze of writings the rural deprived family who is in need of micro credit is always relegated and whose interest we always forget. As a Director of Microfinance company I have visited many rural families in Karnataka to learn how women borrowers make their living, for what they borrow, how they mange their family enterprises, how they repay their loans, how they market their products, how they mange their risks and how they survive in the worst of times. They resort to suicides only as a last resort.

Microfinanancing of rural enterprises need continuous Innovation to reduce the cost of lending all the time. With the digital technology it is easy to reach the rural families and our Organised Banking structure could not innovate in the early days to reach the rural families. Take the micro lending timings. Most of the Self Help Group women meet when they are free form household chorus and if the Credit Functionary wants to meet them the best time is the evening when they can find time after cooking. Women in each village have their set of timing to meet, chit chat and decide. This is just one example of how village women schedule their daily activities and how the Credit Functionary should find the right time to meet them and do business with them. In every aspect of rural credit operations Credit Functionary must be able to innovate and meet the needs of the borrower. Then there are social issues. In some Districts of Karnataka Muslim women were threatened not to borrow because of some diktat from clergy men who oppose borrowing by paying interest! How can the Muslim women survive ? How will the credit operator face such social situations ? Social Innovation is more important than tech innovations in this type of credit operations.

Lending through the Self Help Groups is still the best choice and village women believe in sharing, caring and bonding for mutual wellbeing. This is how the Grammen Bank started its operations based on joint liability of group members both for borrowing and repayment. I was once in Bankapur village in Haveri District of Karnataka and while sitting with the Recovery Officer of Navachetana Microfinance Company who was asking for a member who was absent and whose recovery was due, a Muslim lady member of the SHG came forward to pay her dues because she was sick and could not bring the money. This is how the culture of rural repayment works. In the last decade in many villages the State and Central schemes are promoting all types of SHGs - for tank rehab work, for watershed work and so on. As a result in each village we find many SHGs and the same woman is found in many SHGs. This has led to multiple borrowings and how can one Microfinance Loan Officer will verify the credit worthiness of a woman borrower who is a Member in many SHGs in that village ? Despite the SHG Bank Linkage we still find Multiple borrowings in some villages. (See Tara S Nair, Commercial Micro-Finance and Social Responsibility: A Critique Economic and Political Weekly, July 31st, 2010).

Another issue is linking credit with marketing. Many self employed women are engaged in small economic activities like flower and vegetable, condiments selling, milk selling etc. The Microfinance has to be linked to Micromarketing . Who is to do this? A Loan Officer has to be smart at the village level to be able to target for lending those women who are good in marketing and subsequent repayment. This is here where we need innovation in linking credit with marketing. Many of the Microfinance Filed Officers have to understand these rural nuances and operate, which is not happening at present. Empowerment of the women in the villages is the real business of the business of Microfinance Organisations. Empowerment and inclusive finance should go together-then only it makes sense.

Transparency, Accountability and Responsibility all go together and this is where the big Micro finance Players like the SKS have failed. In 2008-09 Mr Akula got a gross remuneration of Rs 88 lakhs in eight months and Mr Gurmani got Rs. 46.36 lakhs in five months These have been revealed after the Initial Public Offer (IPO) ! Mohamed Yunus calls these IPOs as loan sharks and according to him this is not microfinance (See Business India November 1-14, 2010) We have not seen such things happening in Grameen Bank. In the words of Prof. Jagdish Bhagwati we have to replace Corporate Social Responsibility with Personal Social Responsibility (PSR) because CSR has now been reduced to passing the buck by the CEO's.

Many have argued for better regulation of the Microfinance Companies by the Reserve Bank and the Banks who finance the Microfinance companies.

Rating Agencies in India which rate the Microfinance Institutions are just money makers! Just give them money they will rate you in whatever way you want ! There are many recognised ways of rating like Social Performance Management framework (SPM) developed by Impact Consortium, Progress out of Poverty Index (PPI) developed by Grameen Foundation and Client Protection Principles (CPP) developed by Centre for Financial Inclusion Organisation (See Tara Nair, Commercial Microfinance, EPW July 31 2010.) These six CPPs are (1) Avoid Over- indebtedness, (2) Terms and conditions of borrowings are transparent, (3) Debt collection practices are not abusive or coercive, (4) High Ethical Standards on the part of loan officers while interacting particularly with women borrowers, (5) Timely and responsive complaint resolutions, (6) Privacy of client data, who is borrowing for what etc. The SPM is a process of translating mission into practice, including setting social objectives, tracking social performance and using information to improve practice.

We do not know how many of the Indian Microfinance companies have signed such CPPs or adopted SPM in India. Some of the Microfinance Entities such as Asmitha Microfin and Share Microfin promoted by the Shram family made huge profits by increasing the shareholding of the Chief Promoters and reducing the equity held by the community collectives.

I -TEAR is nothing but adherence to simple principles of ethics, equity, and probity and should become part of the Microfinance Institution's heart and soul. We do not need Regulators to discipline the sector which is based on social conscience. All we need, what Mahatma Gandhi said is a passion to "do greatest good of the greatest number of people" and not the greatest good of the smallest number of Microfinance CEOs and their Directors.

Use of IT in health care: Doubts and benefits

Health tech companies are not sure of the measures to be adopted if high tech instruments fail.

Information technology is now spreading to all sectors of the economy from job creation to education to manufacturing to travel and tourism. Health care of the people is one area where IT is being used in the west to provide better and timely care and also to reduce the cost of care to the patients by avoiding unnecessary hospital visits. Many US based IT companies have developed sophisticated IT and telemedicine for the alzheimer patients like the GPS devices attached to their ankles to track their movements when they are alone. Some of these companies claim that these IT enabled medical technologies have turned the traditional hospital care into proactive patient-centric health care by improving health outcomes and quality of care of the patients.

Patient information can be accessed anytime and anywhere and some image automation software companies like Global Media Group allows clinicians to store and forward digital medical images of eyes, throat and skin. Even committing suicide by swallowing poison or accidental poison effects on family members can be traced quickly by nurses and care givers by poison exposures on phones!

But even in the US, which is a pioneer in the use of IT in health care, problems are many and it still has a long way to go. For the first time in the US, Medicare will soon track the spending on millions of individual beneficiaries to reward hospitals that hold down costs and penalise those whose patients prove most expensive.

Medicare Spending

The US health department plans to establish Medicare spending per beneficiary as a new measure of hospital performance just like the mortality rate of heart attack patients and the infection rate of surgery patients. Under the new health law, Medicare will cut payments to hospitals if they do not replace paper files with electronics health records and it will further reduce payments to hospitals with high rates of preventable errors, injuries, infections etc.

The strategy of health care in the US is to improve the quality and efficiency of people's health by linking payments to the performance of health care providers and is best described by the economists as value based purchasing and will distribute Medicare funds to the hospitals based on this principle.

But there are also serious doubts about the efficacy of the system. If the big financial giants could fudge data and cause global financial crisis, there are doubts whether the IT approach can really bring in good health at low cost in the US. Many of these health tech companies are not sure of the measures to be adopted if these high tech instruments fail to perform or perform wrongly and what should be done and who is responsible for these faults? If the health data is wrongly used or hacked by someone how will the health insurance companies decide on insurance claims and make settlements?

In India many super speciality hospitals in the big cities have developed medical records and IT enabled patient's record keeping. But when we go to the district hospitals and primary health centres in many states the situation is in a mess. Even the basic birth and death registers are still not updated from time to time.

In many of the villages the birth registration of new borns are never done because of social and cultural factors like women delivering her first child in her mother's house/village than in her husband's house/village. The first birth, according to our Indian rural tradition, is supposed to be precious and has to be in her mother's care and house.

The naming of the new born is also done in her mother's house and all this takes as many as six to seven months. Due to these intervals the birth registration is postponed. If the registration is made compulsory in hospitals at the time of birth, the children's progress can be tracked later tracked to their school enrollment, schooling record, drop out if any, till they attain the age of 18.

India should expedite the use of information technology as it can be a great instrument for tracking our human resources' wellbeing. UID is just one IT instrument that the Government of India is promoting. But the real need is to build the IT enabled information system right from the gram panchayats level so that information is available at the click of a mouse.

Job Guarantee—For whom and how?

The Employment Guarantee Scheme of the government can succeed only if the private sector is involved.

The UPA government's main programme for winning the people's goodwill has been the Employment Guarantee Scheme (EGS) for income generation and asset creation for a large majority of the rural poor. It is not for the urban poor though.

There is no partnership of the EGS with the corporate sector. The corporate sector feels that the EGS is a waste of public resources. Dr. Madhav Mehra, President of the World Council for Corporate Governance, says: "The poor in India as consumers can transform the bottomlines of many fading corporations and save them from bankruptcy while making this place a less dangerous place. There is no need for the government to dole out

Rs. 30,000 crore of public money every year in the name of poverty alleviation through employment generation. The same money can be spent on infrastructure, electricity, water and sanitation."

The EGS of the UPA government is on the lines of a similar Maharashtra project. The National Rural Employment Guarantee Act 2004 will not succeed if a partnership with the corporate sector is not built into the EGS. We are living in a globalised world and even rural areas are not free from global effects.

Some Success

Despite many shortcomings in the Maharashtra EGS, the programme did help create some job guarantee, albeit of a temporary nature. It concentrated on public works like road building, breaking stones and quarrying. Contractors hired men and women and paid wages. In the sixties, Maharashtra and Karnataka witnessed a severe drought and the EGS was a re-action to that drought. Roads and stone-quarrying were popular but how long one can break stones and spread mud on village roads? Actually, few public assets were created under the scheme. Public assets like roads, ponds, wells and so on can be created once and not every year! But then, in the last few years, Maharashtra was wise enough to change the thrust towards increasing the value addition of private assets like private lands, by water recharge and moisture conservation. Watershed development enables the creation of private assets for small and marginal farmers.

It was the best achievement of the EGS in Maharashtra and was popularly known as a private-public asset of the EGS programme. We need to have at the village level, good organisational arrangements to get this public-private synergy Are our village panchayats and gram sabhas competent and efficient enough to achieve it?

The government has to adopt a strategy for employment generation in the rural areas with the state and the corporates. There is the question of whom to give employment to—the skilled, the unskilled, women and men. There are also a large number of semi-skilled young men/women. Their employment depends on market opportunities and how then-products fetch market prices. There is a huge number of skilled/semi-skilled people in rural India who also need employment guarantees and for whom the present EGS is not thought of. This is where the corporate sector can play a critical role. Let there be a two-track employment guarantee—one for the unskilled wage labourers who depend on public works and private seasonal farm work, and the other for skilled artisans and workers who can create wealth for the village community. Our handloom workers, potters, carpenters and so on are the wealth creators in rural India. No one thinks of them in the context of the EGS.

Alternative Plan

The Confederation of Indian Industries (CH) is now talking of an alternative plan for job reservations in the private sector, not as demanded by the Government of India, but a plan which would tap the employment generation potential for the disadvantaged sections of society. The CH has kick-started a programme in association with the UK-based City and Guilds Group under which it plans to impart vocational training to one million people in the country.

What the rural poor need is just not an employment guarantee, which is in the nature of wage employment, but also market opportunities to sell "their products". Their unskilled labour is also a "product" which can be re-fined over a period of time and "sold". This is what some corporates have done by buying these "unskilled labour products" from rural areas. ITC's "Farm and Social Forestry Project" effectively leveraged its wood Fibre need to provide income generation for the economically backward wasteland owners in Andhra Pradesh.

There is nothing in the proposed EGS on how the vibrant Stree Shakti groups can be used to provide employment guarantees to women. Many corporates do not know how to leverage gram panchayats and their local knowledge and resources to bring value addition to what the villagers are already doing. Let the UPA government rethink on how to make the EGS a tool not just for doling out money but also for wealth creation in rural India, in partnership with the private sector.

Cash Transfer to India's *Aam Aadmi* and *Aural*: Challenges, Threats and Opportunities

The hot news before the coming Parliament election is the cash transfer to the poor families in rural India instead of ration in kind such as wheat, rice, and kerosene, and towards the wages for the rural works done under the Mahatma Gandhi National Rural Employment Guarantee Programme (MGNREGP).

Indian villages are not easy to understand in terms of their sociology and the economics of their transactions. The latest issue of *The London Economist* (17 Nov. 2012) carries an interesting feature on two villages in Chhattisgarh (Maheshpur) and UP (Kailashpur), and how the BPL (Below the Poverty Line) families are struggling to get their entitlements from the State shops and agencies. The ration cards belong to the two sons of a BPL family head - one has died and the other has moved away from the village, and the father uses these cards to feed himself and the rest of his family. The widow of the dead son is worried about her entitlement when her husband has died. Not all BPL families have cards and some above the BPL have cards and some don't have the cards at all. Theft from anti-poverty programmes — reselling subsidised food and pocketing the difference — is endemic. An investigation by Bloomberg News Agency reckoned that $ 14.5 billion worth of food has been ripped off from the PDS in UP alone in the past 10 years.

So the UPA Government now wants to promote direct cash transfer (DCT) to the poor so that they can buy whatever they want, from wherever they want. Many countries like Mexico, Jamaica, Brazil, Nicaragua, Honduras, and Chile have launched such DCT programmes. Brazil's Bolsa Escola has been highly acclaimed around the world because they hit two birds with one stone — it is a conditional cash transfer to a family of children from 6 to 15 years, when that family will get the cash only if these kids are enrolled in the school. Similarly, families will get cash if the kids are not working in hazardous factories-thus eradicating child labour problems. Why the Indian Government is not promoting conditional cash transfer to the BPL families is a big question??

The Real Picture!

DCT operations are linked to the '*Aadhaar* Card', and this card business has faced enormous problems around the States in Jharkhand and other Pilot States where they are being tested for upscaling around the country. In Jharkhand, as reported by the media (see *The Hindu,* Op-ED, Dec. 2012), one labourer tries eight times placing different fingers in the hope that one will work and keeps going outside the *Aadhaar* office to scrub and wash his fingers and tries again in vain. The *Aadhaar* guy tells him to put *Vaseline* or *Boroplus* on the fingers before going to sleep and come back again! He has worked in MNREGP and his wages are not paid and his biometric goes *fut!* Half of MNREGP workers fingerprints don't match.

The next stage, assuming the *biometrics* clicked, is how the Banking Correspondent (BC) actually pays the amount right at the doorstep of the family of the wage-earner. Villagers are used to deal with village patwaris or Panchayat secretary or the Panchayat *pradhan* for decades. Now this BC is another character who will play havoc with the poor 'aam *admi'* and *'aurat!* Since our public sector banks have failed to reach the villagers in India, they have now floated another rural bureaucrat called BC who will carry what are called Micro-ATMs and pay the villagers. Village post offices were also used to pay the wages, but now these BCs will take over. Because of poor Internet connectivity, the *Aadhar* accounts and Micro-ATMs don't work 24x7x365, as they work in the big cities of India.

The whole *Aadhaar* ID business has received a lot of critical analysis based on the field realities across the country, and like all pre-election announcements by political parties going haywire, the whole DCT approach announced by the Congress will go down in the history of India as "e" disaster if implemented in a hurry. Many critics of DCT have raised as many as six crucial issues which, if not handled well, will land the whole experiment in a limbo (see M Rajshekar, *Six Questions on DCT,* Economic Times, Dec. 13, 2012):

1. Will everyone receive their *Aadhaar* numbers in time?
2. Will everyone be issued bank account in time?
3. Will the last mile Banking Channel be ready in time?
4. Will the UID payment system work flawlessly on scale?
5. Can legitimate beneficiaries like the aged 80+ be excluded?
6. Can the Government identify the poor accurately?

Now India is a Federal State and the last mile problems are critical as they reach the 5.95 lakh inhabitated villages of India - forget about the thousands of urban slums and shanty towns. Indian village Panchayats are now constitutionally mandated, thanks to the 73rd Constitutional amendments. Similarly, urban local bodies are also constitutional entities as per the 74th amendments. Some States have well-developed Panchayats with smart Panchayat Secretaries. Since Panchayat Secretaries are like Chief Secretaries of the State Government at the village level — and they are stationed in the villages - so why not they be made as BCs of the particular Banks instead of an outsider coming as a BC with the Micro-ATM? Every Panchayat should have its own Micro-ATM and if it is not working, they can all protest to the Panchayat Pradhan who is in the village. Unfortunately, neither our Ministers, nor MLAs and MPs, nor our IAS bureaucrats who frame policies wish to strengthen these Panchayats as instruments of good governance. Each Ministry at the Centre and the State wants to establish their own fiefdoms from New Delhi to the last village in India. Let us strengthen the Gram Sabha and Gram Panchayat as our tools to reach the rural India.

6

Environment and the Humans

The WASH Factor in India

India has many adventures in capitalism, but the WASH factor, if not handled urgently, will wipe away our global; glory.

India is leading in demographic dividend and with young population increasing and the migration to the urban space going up in the years to come, the density of the urban space is going to be congested. This would create problems in Water, Sanitation and Health (WASH) for the poor and the rich. The rich somehow manage, but what about the large section of the urban slums and rural areas still left with a large number of farming families, artisans and the elderly? India is now emerging as a Nation with many adventures in capitalism, but lagging behind in WASH — a critical sector for human development. Indian rivers, according to many tests, are rife with diarrhoeal diseases and human faeces are everywhere in hundreds of our villages. Our Ministers and Bureaucrats will never talk of the WASH issues because it is a dirty subject.

Waiting: A Way of Life

I am reminded of the conversation between a smart IAS Officer and Prince Charles who was visiting Kanha National Park in MP. This IAS Officer was escorting the Prince as he was the Guest of the Government of India, and it was late evening (time for open defecation). When they were passing through village streets, many women got up when they saw the car lights. The Prince asked the IAS Officer why these women stood up. "Your Honor, they were all waiting to see you." The Prince said apologetically, "I'm sorry I kept them waiting!" "Don't worry Sir, they're used to this type of waiting!"

This is how our smart bureaucrats fool the visitors to India and avoid talking on toilets, sanitation, handwashing, diseases affecting children, mothers and adolescents. When there is shit all around, we are proud of our growing glory in the world as a Nation with Fortune 500 billionaires! India has many adventures in capitalism, but the WASH factor, if not handled urgently, will wipe away the global glory of India. WASH alone will wipe the tears of many poor families struggling with their livelihoods.

Because of the WASH factor, India has a high incidence of diarrhoeal diseases as in many African countries. According to the WHO, 2.6 billion around the world lack access to a toilet that is not overflowing, affordable, and has a tap nearby to wash their hands. Nearly one billion defecate outdoors because they have no facilities. A majority defecate and walk away! Some at least adopt 'cat methods' afterwards, i.e., cover with sand, mud or soil!

Wake up to WASH

Protected toilet for every family is the answer in India. The Bill and Melinda Gates Foundation plans to spend $266 million over the next five years on toilet initiatives. According to Frank Rijsberman who heads the sanitation effort in the Gates Foundation, toilets can save many lives than any other health device.

Some 22 Universities around the world are working with Gates Foundation to design a toilet that is robust, easy to clean, water and energy self-sufficient, and costs a user less than five cents a day. Unfortunately, none of the Indian IITs or Water-focussed NGOs have ever cared to work on such WASH issues in India, except voluntary agencies such as Sulabh Shauchalaya and Safai Vidyalaya in Gujarat, who have done remarkable work in establishing household and community toilets in many cities of India. Ramakrishna Mission in the Midnapore District of West Bengal did commendable work with the help of UNICEF in popularising household toilets for many poor families. But these were used by them mostly as storage or puja rooms! God is now confined in the toilet!

Indian Railways need better toilets so that they stop spreading the human shit all along the railway lines across the country. Why not the railways adopt toilets as in aircrafts-vacuum-based? *The New York Times* has reported that the bathroom fixtures expert Kohler has now designed an expensive toilet with heated seat, music, a lid that automatically raises and lowers, a remote control and lots of other features. What Indian poor families in villages need is leach pit to save water and convert human excreta into manure for the fields. Will our Ministries of Water Resources and Health, both in the Centre and the States, wake up to push the WASH factor?

Water Goes the Oil Way

Much has been written on water and many have experienced what it is to have less, more, and nothing, of water.

Many in cities panic on water scarcity, and long queues of kids and women in front of non-working public watertaps in urban slums are a common scene. The rich are busy watering their green lawns despite the acute scarcity of water. The old are struggling to shower with small droplets of water. Experts have described the impending water bankruptcy as a crisis far graver than the global financial meltdown. The impact climate change has on water resources is of grave concern as it directly affects agricultural output, sanitation, health and the future of the planet itself. Sanitation and public toilets are the first casualty, and girls and women are the worst sufferers of water scarcity. Patients with water-related diseases like diarrohea and respiratory infections fill half the hospital beds in India and other African countries. Worldwide, dirty water and poor sanitation kill as many as 5,000 kids a day!

But the misuse of water by industries and the luxurious lifestyle of a group of households go on unabated. Paper and pulp industries, cement, aluminum, steel and fertilisers - are all water intensive and misuse water resources in India, reveals the Centre for Science and Environment journal, *Down to Earth,* In 2008-9, these industries together withdrew, about 41,538 million cubic metres of fresh water, equivalent to the fresh water demand of 1.1 billion people on a daily basis! This is a free resource of Mother Earth! In Kerala, the High Court directed the Coca Cola plant to be shut down because the villagers lost their waterbodies like tanks and wells, and we hear such stories across the world on a daily basis. Who is to check the misuse of water by anybody and everybody? In Delhi, 40 per cent of the piped water leaks and goes waste.

The most water-needed activity is farming, and over the years billions of farm borewells have nearly exhausted the underground water table in many parts of farming India. However, there are some novel experiments which provide a ray of hope for the farming community. In Andhra Pradesh, Raja Rao's Bharati Integrated Rural Development Project has launched the Hydrological Budgeting to help farmers grow crops which don't consume too much, water. Such voluntary initiatives can bring better change than the State's regulatory steps.

Given this global situation, what should be done by the State, the individual households, the industries and by each of us before water becomes a scarce commodity like oil? Singapore is a small island country without much land, but is known for its best management of water resources in the world (see *The London Economist* special report on Water, May 22, 2010). Little is wasted in Singapore and used water is treated, reused for industrial purposes or mixed with reservoir water for drinking. Together, recycled waste and desalinated water are expected soon to meet 25-30 per cent of the total demand.

Chennai was the earliest city to impose rainwater harvesting structures for all residential buildings, both old and new. Bengaluru has now followed suit. The Bangalore Water Supply and Sewerage Board (BWSSB) has mandated all residential buildings to get the rainwater harvesting structures installed before the end of June 2010. I have installed both solar water heater system and also the rain water harvesting structures in my home, saving a good amount on electricity and water charges. This rain harvesting technology is now picking up and many masons and plumbers are being trained by NGOs as well as the technology institutes. But if it has to catch up, there is need for real estate companies to implement rainwater harvesting in all new constructions. Only then can rainwater be captured for wider use in a bigger way!

Are Our Cities Livable and Harmonious?

With rising urbanisation, the 21st century is going to be the urban century where cities become the centres of both prosperity and squalour, and the governance of cities become more critical than the governance of the State. Cities occupy only 2 per cent of the worlds land, but consume 75 per cent of its resources. Cities produce close to 80 per cent of all carbondioxide! How do we make them livable and harmonious? How do we make them fit for all generations-the young and the old? How do we tackle slums and integrate the city spectrum? What are those Global City Indicators which can be used with understanding by the city Mayors and Managers? How do we tackle the complexities of land ownership and enhance market to deliver low income housing solutions? These were some of the burning issues passionately debated by thousands of participants like this author from all over the world in the World Urban Forum-4 organised by the UN-Habitat and hosted by the Nanjing City Government in China (Nov. 2008). My attendance was on behalf of the institute of Social Sciences, New Delhi.

The Asian Development Bank which released its flagship report in the conference on "Managing Asian Cities", says that "large cities are more productive than smaller ones and labour productivity generally increases with city size". Another emerging trend is to merge growing small cities by forming them into mega cities on a scafe never seen before - for example, Tokyo-Nagoya-Osaka-Kyoto-Kobe which is likely to have 60 million people by 2015. By 2010 the population of Hongkong-Shenzen-Guangdong mega region could reach 120 million. But these regional tube-like cities need to develop complex systems of coordination of water, transport, communications and infrastructure. Can we develop Tumkur-Bengaluru-Mysore as one mega city region?

Need of a Universal Design

European Countries like Sweden do not like to build big cities and they want towns to come up instead of mega-cities with all the attendant problems of transport and traffic. Swedes want a **Healed Town - a town for everyone.** Everybody should benefit-young, old, the strong, the weak, women, men and children, healthy and sick. Urban Citizens have varying requirements and the same person can require different types of town or urban space during different stages in life, or lifestyles, or values and travel patterns like the cyclists; disabled and those who walk differently. The Swedish experience tells that it is not sustainable to impose an identical pattern on all towns and cities in a country, because each of them is unique with differing needs and dreams. Cities cannot be harrnonious for all unless they adopt what the Norwegian Government calls the Universal Design principle in developing the cities. "Universal design is the design of products and environment ***to be usable by all people*** to the greatest extent possible without the need for adaptation or specialised design."

Design is a common term for all work processes involved in the shaping of the physical world, encompassing community planning, land use, architecture, construction activity, product development and more. Can our cities like New Delhi and Mumbai, Bengaluru and Kolkata emulate any of these global city styles? Cities like New York and London have effective Mayors and hence they are able to make a difference. Where are the Mayors of Mumbai, Bengaluru and Kolkata? Government bureaucrats aided by crony Ministers manage these cities, and no wonder when terrorists hit Mumbai on 26/11, there was no Mayor to come to the rescue of the victims unlike Mayor Rudolph Giuliani of New York who did a remarkable job in helping the victims of 9/11 in New York. Little attention has been paid to the regional and local governance in the development policy of most donor countries, even though strong local government authorities or Municipalities are essential for sustainable development.

Today's urban planning is not just about physical planning of the cities or towns, but it is all about cross-sect oral integration, coordination between different management levels, and active participation by the local population and interest groups, particularly the informal settlement groups like the slum population surrounding most of the cities. Globally speaking, cities cover only 3 pe cent of land altogether, but they leave large ecological footprints. At the same time, human habitats in cities, if properly planned, can relieve the pressure on the same ecosystems. This has been called urban sustainability multiplier, which refers to the process by which high urban sustainability significantly shrinks per capita ecological footprints by reducing energy and material needs. For example, multiple family dwellings reduce the per capita consumption of building materials and services infrastructure. To get this multiplier, we need strong urban local governments and not Urban Ministries.

Brazilian Breeze

Our city planners can learn from Curtiba's excellent transport system.

The thought of a fifteen-hour flight was daunting, specially at the age of 72 But my fears were un founded, the journey from Dubai to Curitiba in Brazil by Emirates went smoothly. The in-flight service was superb and passenger friendly. I drank plenty of fluids, ten liters of water, juice and cocktails, to keep myself hydrated and chatted to the flight attendants about now they handle complaints and emergencies.

On anding, we drove down the streets of Curitiba, the air was fresh and invigorating. In the course of the next one week, was caught up by the enormous enthusiasm of the Brazilians to enjoy life.

I was part of the Indian delegation attending the International Conference on Innovative Cities held from March 10-14 in

Curitiba. The event was organised by the Federation of Industries of the State of Parana in Brazil. Curitiba is a fascinating city known or its famous Bus Rapid Transit System (BRTS). A former mayor of the city, Jaime erner, who built the BRTS held us spellbound with an informative talk on the subject. He spoke like an architect, a city-planner, a philosopher. He demystified urban banning. He passionately taked about thinking of cities not as problems but as solutions. He compared the city to turtle which is big and round and moves slowly. According to him, the transport system should be planned in such a way that the citizens move with ease and pleasure like the turtle.

Today Curitiba's city surface transport system is like the subway. A commuter pays to get into the transit bus and can alight anywhere just as one does in the subway trains. Lerner used interesting phrases, like urban acupuncture, spots where residents can get emergency aid and help, to describe urban planning and city management. He described side-walks and footpaths as portable streets. He thinks the best city is one where one lives close to his or her workplace and avoids a long commute. But with cities growing like monsters this is not always possible, hence ways have to be devised to make commuting a pleasure not a pain.

From Curtiba, I took time off to see the rainforest, this journey by train to Morettes was thrilling. It was in 1880 that Emperor Don Pedro officially laid the railway line which cuts through the thick forests. Rail experts from Portugal had dismissed the idea of building the rail line given the tough terrain. But two Brazilian engineers, Antonio Pereira and Joao Soares, built this railway line in five years. The track passes through 13 tunnels, crosses 30 bridges and several trestles that span huge gorges and cling to cliff walls along the way. The cool breeze wafted in while I sipped my Brazilian coffee, I turned my mind to the rainforest outside and thought how climate change is endangering the life of animals, birds, insects that live in it.

Bangalore City Needs to move from Information Technology (IT) to Garbage Technology (GT)

Here stray dogs (estimated around 30,000) pick up the leftovers, and when shooed away, bite the kids going to school. The two-wheelers and three-wheelers hit the people moving on the walking tracks, and the Traffic police, despite their whistles, appear helpless. This is the Bengaluru, once known for its greenery and walkable roads. The lakes are filled up with drainage dirt and emit foul smell, and dengue and chicken guinea are reported in the media and the Bangalore Brihat Mahanagar Palika (BBMP). Doctors keep denying the media reports and the poor women and kids keep struggling in OPDs of the public hospitals and private clinics.

The biggest 'stink story is the lakes and drains and garbage- its segregation at the source and its disposal - how, where-and when. Let us know the fate of lakes first, as there are many lakes around the city. The Uttarahalli Lake's catchment area and its stormwater drain leading into the lake have been encroached, and the weeds have further choked it, making the lake a septic tank emanating unbearable stench.

When the NGO, Environment Support Group (ESG), filed a public interest litigation against the Bangalore Development Authority (BDA) and the BBMP, a Lake Authority was constituted as directed by the High Court. This will be another Authority like the BDA, doing nothing! There are no dearth of enquires and reports on Bengaluru City on what to do, but nothing has been done and the stench continues. According to one A T Ramaswamy Report of 2007, nearly 2488 cases of lake encroachment covering about 1848 acres of lake area had been made by land-grabbers and builders by fabricating documents.

The Madivala Lake is another beautiful lake near the posh BTM Layout in Bengaluru where the bureaucrats and the rich stay, which has turned into another sewage tank. The State Forest Department gets Rs. 1 crore for maintaining this lake, but the money is spent on removing the weeds and not for overall maintenance!

A Smart City?

Garbage is the enemy of lakes, drains and what have you. The city is now sitting on a huge stock of garbage and as per rough estimates, around 4000 tonnes of garbage is generated daily and the contractors have used the now famous Mandur village for dumping the waste. The villagers have been protesting because people are dying of respiratory infections as a result of polluted and infested air and water.

The new Commissioner of BBMP, Rajnesh Goel, an IAS bureaucrat, is struggling to make the segregation at the source as the new 'mantra' for garbage disposal, i.e., at the household level. But what about the final disposal - where and how with what outcomes? Boston city in the US is generating energy with the city garbage. Why not Bengaluru?

The biggest problem of Bengaluru is its governance. Despite the BBMP being a constitutional body as per the 74th Constitutional amendment, where the Mayor and its councilors are like the Chief Minster and MLAs, the Mayor is elected only for one year. Why not a full term of five years to show results? Why not the Chief Minster's and Prime Minister's tenure also for one year?

The late Prime Minister Rajiv Gandhi was a visionary and brought these 73rd (rural local bodies like Panchayats) and 74th (urban local bodies like BBMP) amendment to make them instruments of effective governance. But the Chief Ministers of the States do not empower them with funds, functionaries and functions. The success of London Olympics was in large part due to the effectiveness of the Mayor of London. Look at our Commonwealth Games in New Delhi! There was no Mayor of Delhi in that, but Suresh Kalmadi managed it well to go to jail later!

Years back there was Bangalore Agenda Task Force, where the corporate leaders were thinking of making Bengaluru not just a technology hub but also a livable city, and the Ministers were looking towards the corporate sector for help and support. Look at IBM Smarter Cities project in Rio De Janeiro, Berlin, Beijing, Dublin, Singapore and New York, where they have used the knowledge of technology for crime detection and road safety issues. The IBM Tech Guru Gurudath Banaver says, "The IBM Real Time Crime Centre in New York has brought down the crimes in the city of New York to a great extent." (Read Scott Anthony, *The New Corporate Garage,* Harvard Business Review, Sept. 2012).

Why not the BBMP leaders invite the Global Tech leaders already in the electronics city of Bengaluru to come out and thrash out solutions for the garbage problems of the city? The only dialogue the Commissioner of BBMP is having is with the garbage contractors on where to dump, and not with the garbage technology experts on how to generate energy and make Bengaluru clean and livable!

Corporate Sustainability through Green Leadership

Ever since the Indian constitution passed the 73rd and 74th Constitutional amendments to fulfil the dream of the late Prime Minister Shri Rajiv Gandhi to empower the local bodies in India almost two decades back, the local governments both in the urban and rural India have remained in doldrums because of the lack of the commitment by the politicians in the Parliament and State Assemblies. These commitments are in the nature of providing three Fs-Functions, Functionaries and Funds. All the three Fs are either missing or given from the left hand and taken away by the right hand.

We have today as many as 9,75,000 women panchayat members in the rural parts of India and out of them as many as 8,50,000 belong to the marginalized groups like Scheduled Caste and Scheduled Tribes. India has now taken a bold step to increase the number of seats for women in panchayats to 50 per cent. We have elected leaders from Vidhan Sabha to Lok Sabha and to Rajya Sabha who are incapable of steering India towards growth and poverty. That is why Manatma Gandhi felt the need to build leadership from the bottom up in India i.e., from Gram Sabha (Village Panchayat) to the Vidhan Sabha (State Assembly) and on to the Lok Sabha. Mahatma Gandhi also felt the need for A Strong Leadership Pipe Line for India and in such a pipe line local body leaders and local governance play a vital role in shaping up the Country.

India is now on a global path and given the diversity and complexity of the country, local governance has to be strengthened. We hear a lot about the work done by the Mayor of New York and Mayor of London. But we hardly hear anything from the Mayors of Mumbai, Bengaluru, Kolkatta, because there are no Mayors elected in these Mega cities. Even if they are elected, they remain just for an year as Show pieces without being involved in city planning, management and protection.

When New York faced 9/11 tragedy, it was the Mayor of New York Mr. Gulliani who took charge of the entire situation. When the Taj Hotel in Mumbai was hit by terrorists, there was no Mayor of Mumbai to take charge of the situation. It was a panic situation handled by the Chief Minister of Maharashtra without knowing what to do.

We need in the context of global climate change, the local bodies in India to be empowered and entrusted with the task of managing WE HELP AGENDA, which means tackling WATER, ENERGY, HEALTH, EDUCATION, LABOUR AND PENSION. In the words of Noble prize winner in economics Dr. Paul Krugman, WE HELP AGENDA is now being implemented vigorously by President Obama in the US. Indian local bodies are best suited to tackle WE HELP, because they are very close to the nature where in the words of Daniel Goleman these local leaders have more "Ecological Intelligence". Ecological refers to an understanding of organisms and their ecosystems, and intelligence connotes the capacity to learn from experience and deal effectively with our environment. (See Daniel Goldman, Ecological Intelligence, Broadway Books, New York, 2009)

Let us examine water issue which is critical to India's survival. The village panchayat of Plachimada in Kerala in 2004 and 2005 underwent water scarcity because of the Coco-Cola bottling plant located in Plachimada. With the factory running at full tilt, it saw up to eighty-five truckloads of Coke drive off daily, each bearing more than ten thousand bottles. The agitation by the local villagers continued for years and Coke plant drew its water from a deep aquifer. In the analysis showed by the villagers, it was revealed that 200 liters of water to grow the sugarcane crop goes into one liter of coke. Thanks to the agitation of the Plachimada villagers and the village panchayat. Coco-Cola installed a sophisticated rain water harvesting system designed to recharge ground water sources. This one illustration goes to show how water is a critical resource and the corporate sector cannot take it for granted as a free resource available. According to the latest Economist, India is the world's biggest user of ground water, with some 20 millions bore holes providing water for over 60 per cent of it's irrigated area. The local bodies are the ones, who know the local water problems cutting across village wells, tanks, ponds and various water harvesting sources at the village levels. World Bank has spent billions of dollars in India for water harvesting and tank rehabilitation programmes. But they all have not involved local bodies in a big way. This is where the green leadership of local bodies assumes importance and it has remained a missed opportunity. When Mr. Digvijay Singh was the Chief Minister of M.P. he launched what was then called Pani Rokho programme involving the entire village community including village Panchayat under the Rajiv Gandhi Watershed Mission in the State. The water harvesting technologies were all understood by making simple slogans like Khet Ka Pani Khet Me (Rain fallen in the Farm should remain in the Farm. Ghar Ka Pani Ghar Me (Rain Fallen in the house top should remain in the house etc.) Now there are so many parallel bodies in India who are engaged in water protection issues and as a result the Local Bodies in India both in the urban and rural areas have been bypassed.

Energy is another important area where local bodies can do wonders. The emerging energy technologies viz. wind energy, solar energy etc., are romanticised by the National Level Planners and Experts. Whatever wind energy infrastructure has been created in India, it is done without involvement of the local bodies. In Bengaluru lot of Solar Systems are installed by the residents and I am one of them. The Bengaluru Electric Supply Company gives me a discount of Rs. 40 every month in my electricity consumption, because I have installed Solar System. This is a good step. If all our local bodies in India are trained and educated on the virtues of wind and solar energy systems and if our corporate leaders in energy sector sit down with the local bodies and make them as the stake holders we can see a big revolution in India.

The Corporate Sector can play a vital role in strengthening the local governance in India by entering into partnership for installation of renewable energy systems. The power of renewable energy system is going to be very critical in the coming century and the corporate sector involved in generating Solar and Solar Photovoltaic Energy, Thermal Power, Wind, Ocean Wave Power, Fuel Cells, Compressed Air Systems are all going to be developed in a big way around the world by energy enterprises. China today currently meets 7.7 per cent of its energy needs from renewable sources and it is going to raise to 15 per cent by 2020. In India despite two decades of liberal incentives to the wind mills, their plant load factor (pit) is still 11.7 per cent and only the turbine makers and the investors have been benefited. We still do not know about the payments made to wind farm developers how much power they have fed to the grid The non performing Ministry of Renewal Energy has just continued to provide accelerated depreciation to wind turbines virtually allowing investor to write off its capital in a year - a ten year tax holiday - all without generating any wind power!

Thomas Edison hundred years back felt that the best way to meet customers needs would be to set up network of decentralised power plants in or near homes or offices. The bright new hope is the micro power (wind and solar) in countries like India and these local bodies can play a good role only if the Corporate sectors work with them. Just as we need decentralised energy systems, we also need decentralised local and efficient governance system.

Health is another area where the local bodies in India are not involved in a big way. Here again the parallel public structure of the state bypasses many of the local bodies, particularly, in the rural areas where panchayatas can do wonderful work for reducing maternal and child mortality by effective immunisation and family spacing programmes. In the years to come certain public health diseases like HIV/AIDS, Influenza Pandemic are all going to be biggest public health threats.

Education, particularly the primary and basic education is still for away from the target of 100 per cent literacy in the rural areas, and the women's literacy is still worst. A school teacher in a typical village in India is still not answerable to the panchayat president. Indian politicians always quote the example of Mayor of New York, who has brought the school system in New York city to perform and show results in the learning levels of the kids in the city, particularly the marginalised groups like the Hispanics, African-Americans etc. The big cities in India like Mumbai, Bengaluru, Kolkatta where educational enterprises are making money are not bothered to universalize basic education in the slums of these cities. The Urban local bodies of these cities can do great work if they are involved in a systematic manner.

Labour in India is still young and the demographic dividend will not lead to increased GDP if 70 per cent of the rural labour is not productively employed. The biggest successful employment programme in India is the National Rural Employment Guarantee Programme (NREGP) which has provided 100 days of employment to the rural poor and the rural infrastructure like village roads, village ponds, village water harvesting structures have all been improved by employing this productive labour. The local panchayats have been involved in this NREGP to a great extent although there is scope for involving them more systematically way by making them accountable for employing the eligible labour on productive works. Here again the corporate sector has not extended it's hand in generating much more employment and there is now a talk to extend NREGP to provide technical training to the rural youth so that they can improve their talent for productive employment in the corporate sector.

Pension for the old and the disabled in India has been tackled by half a dozen state level and federal level departments of social welfare and the Ministry of Labour. Although the Information Technology has helped to generate lot of wealth in India among the urban intellectuals, this technology has not penetrated the rural hinterland to bring in more prosperity on par with the urban India. Very recently the Prime Minister Dr. Manmohan Singh said that only 15 per cent of the Indians have health insurance coverage. How should we provide the best health coverage for the I billion Indians ?

7

Looking Forward

In the preceding Development Musings we have captured thoughts ranging from ecology to environment to technology and the emerging global and national scenario of men, women and matters, which can make a profound difference to the wellbeing of people and the planet. The future is a mixture of gloom and hope-gloom because the climatology and the environmental issues are going to be more critical and complicated for handling by our leaders who lack forethought and transparent behaviour. India will have leadership deficit in the years to come and the emerging talent will be attracted more towards wealth generation and innovation than towards public leadership to drive the nation towards prosperity and wellbeing of the poor. As the demographic dividend gets reduced the health care of the elderly will assume greater importance despite the health of the young population playing a critical role. Technology will play a critical role not just in globalisation but also in health care of the young and the old. As reported in The Economist of London

(1st Dec. 2012) "With the help of Medical tricorder-a hand held computer with a detachable sensor, will enable people to diagnose a set of 15 conditions, including diseases as varied as pneumonia, diabetes, without having to rely on a Doctor or a nurse. Ultimately this is all about democratising health care around the world. There are six billion Mobile phones in use around the world and some health care organisations send out text messages to patients reminding them to take medicines, renew their prescriptions or visit a Doctor. With a shortage of Doctors around the world and with increasing aging population, these medical devices will replace the doctors to a large extent."

"But not all Doctors are happy with these gadgets. According to Price Water House physicians do not want patients to become independent and too empowered and health care is a very paternalistic industry. Doctors may be reluctant to use data collected by patients and raising the questions of legal liability if something is missed. According to some experts the Doctor is more comfortable with the liability in a system that does not have rich data than in a system that does have a rich data. In the coming days and years medicine is becoming more of an information science, where simple tasks could be taken over by patients, which could free up Doctors for more demanding problems".

The Health, Education, Labour and Pension (HELP) will be emerging as more critical in the years to come in India because of our demographic landscape. India's public health system is still to go a long way to help our young mothers to deliver safely, which alone can bring down our birth rates and infant mortality rates significantly. Our primary schools in many States are still struggling to get good learning through good teachers, good sanitation to attract the girls from the rural hinterlands. The flagship Mahatma Gandhi National Rural Employment

Guarantee across the country has helped to get better employment for the rural poor but it has to a go a long way to link it up with many other rural livelihood, improvement programmes like food entitlements, housing and others. Cash transfers are controversial because of several hurdles in identifying the poor who are entitled for them despite the claims made for Adhar as the proof of identity of the rural poor.

Rural India is a place with diversity of religion, occupation and livelihoods and with urban migration the scenario will change and the technology-from Mobile phones to online banking to Micro-ATMs - will become more widespread leading to more migration and depriving precious labour for farming. The old will remain in the villages, whose pension and health will become more worrying for the policy makers and techies alike.

Another critical trend will be the status of women not just at home but in a large context of the nation building and pushing the global economy to greater heights. With better education and improved domestic status, women would assert their role more effectively despite the prevalence of dangerous anti women social forums like the Khap Panchayats in Haryana (India). The 21st century should become the Century of the women ! Many women's forum have been emerged around the world to protect them from sex scandals, from maltreatment in work places and homes which is a positive trend.

WASH (Water and Sanitation and Health) factor is going to be worst in the years to come in India because of mismanagement of water resources, leading to bad sanitation and its effect on public health of the urban and the rural poor. According to WHO and UNICEF over 600 million Indians defecate in the open. In UP alone hardly 20 per cent of its population have toilets of their own. Our Political leaders instead of providing free TVs and Laptops should provide protected toilets to all the rural families. Women and girls are the worst affected-physically and psychologically - by this appalling lack of toilets. They are the ones who are forced to go to isolated spots mostly in the dark, which makes them vulnerable to molestation and rape and attacks from wild animals.

Then comes the energy for the poor both in urban and rural India for their living. According to the Census of India of the 236 million households as many as 31 per cent use kerosene and the rest use the electricity from the grid. Several attempts have been made to provide solar lamps and systems to those rural poor who are in the "dark" and get rid of the kerosene syndrome. Some Innovators like the SELCO in Karnataka have made great contribution to lit the light in the poor households by providing solar lamps for kids to read and mothers to cook and to reach as many as 135,000 rural families. But the scale is a long way to go.

Decades ago the Management Guru Late Prof CK Pralhad brought out the concept of customers (people) at the bottom of the pyramid, to maximize the sale of products by several enterprises, whose purchasing power will not be high but they form a huge consumer market. We have to use the same concept for reaching out the poor in India who form the bottom of India's Pyramid who have to be reached with policies and programmes for improving their quality of life. But the politicians always reach them for votes but not for providing a better quality of life. This is going to be the biggest challenge in the years to come not just in India but in many countries like Africa and the Middle East.

More than half of Indians are at the bottom of India's Pyramid and they are to be uplifted not by slogans and goodies but by providing livelihood opportunities and basic goods and services for their wellbeing. That is the challenge of the 21st Century India.

Karnataka's New Government: Led by a 'Good Shepherd'?

Now that Karnataka has a new Chief Minister (CM) in Siddaramaiah, people in the State heaved a sigh of relief from the bitter corruption and mudslinging among the leaders. The citizens were sick of leaders without a human face and a human touch. Now that the Congress has chosen a passionate leader as CM, will he lead the State as a Good Shepherd? To describe him so is itself a tribute to his leadership qualities. Will he practice leadership or shepherd-ship or both? Lord Christ was named a 'Good Shepherd' because he led his followers to enjoy peace and harmony. His followers were described as sheep because they followed their Shepherd with devotion and loyalty and whatnot.

Will the newly elected MLAs follow this Good Shepherd and allow him to do good things for the betterment of the people of Karnataka, particularly those at the bottom of the pyramid in the State? Will the citizens of Karnataka see better days in the years to come or the Good Shepherd will be hit hard from the back? As a social engineer, he had launched in Karnataka what was called AHINDA—a movement for the upliftment of a/pa *sankhyak* or minorities, *hinduligas* or backwards and dalits. In fact, it was late Dev Raj Urs, CM of Karnataka in the 70s, who was behind the AHINDA spirit. Now as a Good Shepherd, the present CM has to convert it as a programme of the Government and implement it.

The CM, before taking his oath of office, went to the statue of the 12th century Saint Basaveshwara in Bengaluru, and garlanded it. That day (May 13, 2013) was coincidently the 'Basava Jayanti' celebrated all over Karnataka. Thus he has started with sacred blessings and his tenure would be watched with vigilance and great expectations Elections come and go, but some good deeds by our leaders are remembered forever. Followership is equally important in a democracy, but a good leader has to inspire the followers. The newly elected CM announced sops worth Rs. 4,409 crore even when there was no full-fledged cabinet to decide such issues, and some MLAs were upset with this decision!

Good Governance

This new government has to grapple with at least five major governance issues in Karnataka:

- **Human Development issues.** such as primary healthcare, primary education, water and sanitation, shelter and skill development for the young, and jobs for the emerging youth are going to be very critical. The NEETS (Not Employed, Educated and Trained) are increasing in Karnataka. Loan waivers are easy, but getting skilled jobs for the NEETS belonging to SC/ST community is difficult and critical.
- Bring out every year the '**Karnataka Human Development Report**' to tell its citizens what they have achieved in terms of human development and wellbeing of the poor and the neglected. This cannot be done by the bureaucrats of the State sitting in Vidhan Soudha, but a Think Tank of eminent people have to come together and do it on behalf of the Government.
- Late Rajiv Gandhi dreamt of **a strong, decentralised governance** from the village panchayats to the top of the structure, and he pushed the 73rd and 74th constitutional amendments to strengthen local government structures like the panchayats in the rural areas and the urban municipal bodies. But the MLAs and MPs and Ministers never delegated funds, functions and functionaries (3-Fs) to these bodies. Can the Good Shepherd do this aggressively?

- Bengaluru city is now the dirtiest in the world and stray dogs, filth and garbage are creating many health th problems for the citizens, (see *my Musings, December* 2012) The Mayor of Bengaluru has to be empowered by making his/her tenure for five years to show results, and the Good Shepherd should help the Mayor with the 3-Fs.
- The **State Planning machinery** should be revamped to make it a body to provide VIM (Vision, Inspiration and Momentum) and not just a bureaucratic body to talk of economics, statistics, GDP and poverty ratio!
- **Maoists, Mines and Murthys: Can We Bring Them Together?**

Tribal areas in India were once the privilege of working in such areas feel sad over the deteriorating living standards of the tribal's and the emergence of terrorist groups in these areas.

As the UNICEF representative of the then undivided Madhya Pradesh, I had the pleasure of visiting Bastar in the early 90s to implement the Mother and child immunisation' Programme. The tribal's were known for their hospitality and they accepted the immunisation, more than in the non-tribal areas. Besides, I also enjoyed their dishes offered the visiting officials of both the government and international, development agencies like 5 the UNICEF. Mangoes in thousands would fall to the ground and mothers would pick them and feed their kids to ensure vitamin replenishment. Minor forest produce like *Mahua* seeds would be sold and the forest department would give them a pittance for their hard work. Forest department officials would make money and deny the rights of the tribals for the forest wealth.

Over a period of time forest wealth in Bastar went down and the tribals lost their rights over the minor forest products the thus the young tribals, who could not go to school, could not build their skills, could not get jobs anywhere, took up guns to fight back the government employees! Forest resources could have been used to set up smallscale industries employing the tribal youth. For example, Companies like *Godrej* could have been invited to set up mango processing plants to boost up the employment of tribal youth and also make money. Instead, the big companies were given licence to dig mines, displacing the tribal and affecting their farming and livelihoods.

The Gram Sabha Members (Tribals) are called to play football and get their signature consenting for mining and displacing them form their land and forest. Big public sector companies like SAIL have polluted the rivers in the tribal belt and the drinking water is now called 'Lal Pani' (Red water).

What went wrong? Why are the tribals up against politicians corporate guys, police and the bureaucrats? Why are they kidnapping and killing politicians and those who are supposed to bring development to them? The Chhattisgarh Government launched what was called Salwa Judum – a civilian military outfit created by the government aimed at countering naxalite/Maoist violence, which was declared as unconstitutional by the Supreme court and was disbanded.

How come the forest department and several department of the government like tribal education, tribal health, over a period of time failed to implement the many development schemes of the government? Young boys and girls dropping out of school and wandering ground without jobs for livelihood – all contributed over a period of time for the simmering frustration and anger by the emerging tribal youth in these areas. The BDOs, and village level functionaries never stayed in the tribal villages. There was no development dialogue between the government functionaries and the tribals – youth, women and the growing.

Corporate Takeovers

Then the corporate leaders like Vedanta in Odisha started digging the mines and displacing the tribals, who lost their livelihoods and had nowhere to go. They took up arms – the only way to show their strength. Thanks to the intervention of the Supreme Court, Vedanta has been asked to consult the Gram Sabhas as per the Forest rights Protection Act. Corporate leaders like Anil Agarwal of Vedanta and Infocian Narayana Murthy, according to harish Kare – a former media Advisor to the Prime Minister – have to set high standards of ethic and morality in dealing with the stakeholders wherever they operate. Otherwise Maoists will take over Murthys! This is just a journalistic phrase according to me! (See harish khare- 'The Murthys and Maoists', *The Hindu,* June 6, 2013)

Narayana Murthy is the symbol of ethics in corporate India, and through various corporate forums he should send the message of handholding to the tribals in India so that they put down their guns and get jobs in various industries that come up in the tribal and non-tribal areas. Unfortunately, the industry groups like Vedanta did not care about the stakeholders like tribals, and worried more about the stakeholders like tribals, and worried more about their shareholders! Result is the emergence of Maoists.

Can the Maoists be turned into shareholders of Vedanta? Why not? Give the tribal youth the skills of mining, give them technical training and absorb them in the mining enterprise. They will put down their guns. But who will initiate these processes? The state government has to do it. The Home Ministry, both at the Centre and the State, Think only of fighting back the Maoists than initiating development dialogue with them. The government thinks only of treating 'arms with arms', which will not work. Maoists have become NEETS (Not Educate, Employed, Trained) and they need skills, jobs and protected livelihoods so that they can put down their guns with honour and lead live with peace.

Evergreen Prof. Manu Kulkarni

We deeply regret to inform, the author breathed his last before he could see the publication. Prof. Manu Kulkarni was known to us as an erudite academician who was capable of simplifying complex phenomenon into easy to read prose. In 2011 October he was in Mumbai to receive Dignity Dialogue Excellence Award in writing. Very affable and effusive, Prof. Kulkarni will be deeply remembered by all at *Dignity Dialogue* and our Bengaluru chapter of Dignity Foundation.

Index

L

M

N

O